PRAISE FOR
INSPIRATIONAL
INFLUENCERS

"It is so easy to feel alone on our journeys these days, and even easier to think about giving up when things get tough. That is exactly why you need a copy of *Inspirational Influencers* – and grab a copy for your best friend! Kim Somers Egelsee and Susie Augustin, together with 23 influential leaders, have shared their toughest stories and triumphs to inspire their readers to keep going even in the most difficult times. Plus, you will find powerful tips at the end of each chapter that each author uses regularly to improve their lives. The curtains are being pulled back so we can all see what top leaders do to live their greatest lives – and it might not be what you think!"

~ Ursula Mentjes, Award Winning Author and Entrepreneur

"Kim and Susie have produced yet another visually stunning layout of soulful, practical, real and personal stories that are not only expansive and enriching for any up-and-coming influencer, but also are a heartfelt embrace of life's deep challenges and personal growth triumphs. The contributing authors in this hot new collab are an A-list of emerging leaders rocking their lives and ambitions. *Inspirational Influencers* book is totally worth your time and energy, and will absolutely lift you to your next levels."

~ Laura Jane, The Yoga Muse

"This book is filled with engaging and impactful real life stories. Each one ultimately leading to profound and invaluable life lessons that everyone will relate to. Once you start reading Inspirational Influencers, you won't want to put it down, and once you finish it you'll want to read it again!"

~ Eden Sustin, Physical Medium and Host of Talk Purpose and Truth Podcast *(with Kim Somers Egelsee)*

"Inspirational Influencers is an excellent book for becoming motivated and inspiring bravery and courage! I highly recommend it."

~ Kyle Wilson, Founder of Jim Rohn Int. and KyleWilson.com

"The level of your influence is determined by the level of your soulful engagement. A true influencer is not a person judging their worth by likes, but a person that has overcome life's obstacles, stayed true to their calling and encourages us to do the same. They have a meaningful message burning in their hearts and a willingness to pick us up and show us the way. By having the confidence and courage to share their dark moments and victories, they free us from our overthinking and empower us to really go for it. We all need more belief, positivity and inspiration to nudge us from our comfort zones and I feel Susie and Kim have gathered the best of the best in this book to help us paint the vision of our biggest dreams and take purposeful action."

~ De'Anna Nunez, High Performance Hypnotist, Author & Speaker

INSPIRATIONAL INFLUENCERS

Transforming Challenges Into
CONFIDENCE
& SUCCESS

SUSIE AUGUSTIN
KIM SOMERS EGELSEE

GET
BRANDED
PRESS

Get Branded Press
Huntington Beach, CA 92648
www.GetBrandedPress.com

ISBN 978-1-944807-07-8 paperback
ISBN 978-1-944807-08-5 ebook
Library of Congress Cataloging-in-Publishing Data is available upon request.

Printed in the United States of America

First Printing, 2019

Edited by Taylor Augustin www.GetBrandedPress.com

Cover & Interior Design by Kate Korniienko-Heidtman

DEDICATION

This book is dedicated to
YOU!
Allow yourself to be inspired and empowered
by these stories
and be willing to take steps
to live your most powerful life,
where you can then
inspire others around you!

ACKNOWLEDGMENTS

Special thanks to our co-authors for being brave enough to be vulnerable and authentic, sharing personal stories and challenges, with the purpose of helping others to dare to shine their brightest light!

Kandice Astamendi, Kathy Bair, Joe Casas, Xiomara Escobar, Anush Gagua, Lisa Giannini, Bonnie Gruttadauria, Lynn Heubach, Barbi Jolliffe, Jazzy Juice, Angela Merchain, Maria Mizzi, Vance Mizzi, Janet Norraik, Elena Planas-Sena, Anita Salazar, Lola Salazar, Mike Somers, Shawna Strong Pierce, Mary Kasparian Sushinski, Harriette Tapia, Melissa Tori, Tara Vevante.

Our deepest gratitude to Kate Korniienko-Heidtman, our talented graphic designer – for our fabulous book covers and branding of Get Branded Press, Sexy, Fit & Fab, 10+ Life – and for our clients' book covers, interior layouts, and eye-catching social media graphics.

Thank you to our videographer Marco Elorreaga of GhettoRig Productions and to The Hotel Huntington Beach for your support and encouragement.

TABLE OF CONTENTS

INTRODUCTION

"I believe that God has put gifts and talents and ability on the inside of every one of us. When you develop that and you believe in yourself, and you believe that you're a person of influence and a person of purpose, I believe you can rise up out of any situation."

~ Joel Osteen

A true partnership when working together is when you both can support, uplift and encourage one another to soar. It is when you each do equal work and contribute in different unique ways, where it fits just like a puzzle and completes each project. It is a unification of minds, energy and purpose melded together to create magic and inspiration. This is what we have, and how this book came about.

While planning what projects we would work on in 2019, we had an inspired idea. Bring together a group of inspirational entrepreneurs who are making a difference in the world, and create a book of shared stories of transforming challenges into confidence and success. We incorporated our Speaking & Writing to Wow! workshops to help them brand themselves as inspirational influencers and experts in their industries, enabling them to make a bigger positive impact in the world.

We have always been great together at doing what Napoleon Hill talks about. When opportunity comes, we step up, select and plan what we want, put it into action, and follow through with persistence. The passion guides and pulls us and makes it all flow toward positive outcomes. At times we create our own opportunities and jump into them, think outside the box and just go for it.

We have been blessed to be friends and soul sisters who have worked together for almost ten years now. There are those people you meet where the synergy just naturally flows and pulls you toward the same mission. This is not an accident, which is why over the years we have been a part of over ten books together, numerous red carpet book launches, hosting two web series together, radio and TV shows, workshops, and masterminds all with the intent and passion to inspire others, ourselves and to make a difference in the world living by example, writing, speaking and teaching. Therefore, it makes all the sense in the world for this book to involve amazing authors with powerful stories and be called *Inspirational Influencers; Transforming Challenges Into Confidence and Success.*

What does it mean to be inspirational, to inspire? To inspire is the ability to communicate a message on a personal level. It means to spark ideas, creativity and belief in others. Making a connection by engaging with others, while leading by example. Impacting others while being passionate about your purpose can be very powerful, allowing optimism to change perception; roadblocks become challenges that can be conquered.

If you study personal development, you may have heard phrases such as *the greater the opposition, the greater the growth and opportunities.* In this book, you'll read about authors who have had tremendous confidence and growth through obstacles, and success stories of triumph over challenges. Based on the content of the author's stories, we've structured the book into 5 categories: Creative Inspiration, Carpe Diem, A Catalyst for Change, Courage, and Confidence.

Do you have a similar story in you? What is holding you back from sharing your story? Allow this book to inspire you to take bold action – on defining your life purpose, following your dreams, and finding work-life balance. We challenge you to speak success and creativity into your life ... to inspire and influence others. We dare you to take action to reach your destiny.

Imagine living a life filled with confidence and courage. Let people see the greatness in you. Get a vision for it, have faith, and change your life today!

We hope you love this book.
Cheers!
Susie and Kim

Huge shifts,

POWERFUL
POSITIVE
CHANGES,

WONDROUS
OPPORTUNITIES

will be presented to you when you get in tune with
who you are, what you truly want, when you are open to it
and why you want to live your best life ever.

~ Kim Somers Egelsee

CREATIVE INSPIRATION

Vincent Van Gogh said, "If you hear a voice within you say 'you cannot paint,' then by all means paint, and that voice will be silenced." What inspires you creatively? Do you practice exerting your perfect and greatest self-expression? What encourages you? Is it music, movies, memories, or magic? Is it when you feel alive, exhilarated, or fascinated by something or someone? Have you thought about it? Most of us just monotonously and robotically push through life, getting through each day. How is that working for you?

We can all use creative inspiration in our lives to uplift, flow, feel meaning, and follow our passions and calling. We need to find meaning in all we do. This involves self-inventory, personal and spiritual development, taking enthusiastic action, and tuning into what makes you excited such as music, travel, photography, fitness, yoga, helping others, art, theatre, nature and more. It involves daring to know your true self inside and out.

YOU can impact the world with your unique talents. Wouldn't you love to live a life of creativity and prosperity, motivating others to also follow their true passion? Embrace your courage and express your talent and creativity. Trust yourself and let people see the greatness in you.

Some of the ways you can find creative inspiration continuously is to practice meditative journaling, sketching or doodling, painting, visualization, combining all of these into vision journaling and vision boards. Creative Inspiration will help you gather new insights and ideas, new ways of thinking and problem solving, and can help you express and cope with feelings. It helps you be in a state of childlike wonderment and joy, and connects you to source, the earth, the universe and the divine. This is true creative inspiration.

VISUALIZE YOUR LIFE BECOME IT, SHARE IT

by Lynn Heubach

I am living my dream! It's 1981. The song, "Every Little Thing She Does is Magic" by Police, is popular on the radio. Prince Charles and Lady Diana are getting married. And even better... I'm finally living in Paris, France for a year while I advance my Foreign Studies at the American University of Paris. I get to share this experience with my roommate and my best friend forever (BFF), Beth.

I had been very successful with my university studies and had been studying foreign languages since I was 12 years old. I had an ear and talent for learning languages and was highly inspired by my dad. My dad was the type who was successful at nearly everything, talented in music, art and business. He owned several businesses, was an engineer, a musician and an artist.

When I was really young in grade school, I remember my dad would take us out to international cuisine restaurants. He could seemingly speak a little bit of every language at each ethnic restaurant. I was in awe of my dad and my next sense, taste, was being developed. I wanted to learn to speak different languages too. I loved tasting different foods because it literally transported me to their world in conjunction with the sights, sounds and nice people who worked and frequented those restaurants. I'd dream of traveling and living abroad, speaking many languages, dancing around and having friends from around the globe.

I was so inspired by the cuisines that I learned how to cook international foods by the age of 11. I started having social gatherings with my friends at our houses in grade school. By the age of 12, I started studying French and Spanish offered at my school. My close friends in school studied languages, too. Some of us worked in our parents' businesses to earn extra money so that we could create our own dinner groups and make plans to travel abroad. We were our own little community of confident, inspiring teenagers.

At the age of 15, because I had been an excellent student of languages, I received the gift to travel to Spain and other parts of Europe with my dad. I was amazed by the diverse cultures, foods and people. My spoken Spanish was not perfect, but I applied myself. When I returned home, I immersed myself further into my studies so that I could graduate early and live abroad to improve my languages and experiences.

In January 1978, I met a foreign exchange student, Beth, from Brazil in my French class. We soon became BFF's. She relocated with our family as my Exchange Sister in Covina, CA. We had so many things in common. We soon began to enroll and inspire our families to allow me to go live with Beth's family in Brazil, since I was scheduled to graduate early from high school. My challenge at the time was getting really immersed in my studies and not get too distracted. My goal was to successfully graduate a full year early; however, that did not happen. I graduated a semester early. My senior semester comprised of two classes. The rest of the time I worked at my dad's business and saved a lot of money for my future travels.

My biggest challenge in studying and speaking languages was that no one in my family did, nor did any of my friends or neighbors. I had to figure this all out on my own and find opportunities to practice speaking. My ancestors date back to the signing of the Declaration of Independence. No one in my family ever traveled abroad (except my dad when he was in the Navy during WWII). I was the youngest of four children raised in a divorced household. My desire for foreign tastes was first with food at the restaurants, and when I closed my eyes, I dreamed I was eating at a kitchen table as a family in a different country where we were all talking in different languages. I loved the sounds of different music, dances and ways of being. Looking back, I created in my mind living abroad with different families. And so, it came to be.

Again, my challenge was that I was from an all-American family with no ties to different languages or foreign travel. I did everything possible in my studies, savings and actions to make sure I enrolled my parents in my future path. My dad inspired me, so I inspired him back too.

With each year of study and application of languages, my confidence and opportunities grew. Fast forward to January 1979, I just turned 18 and it's "Saturday Night Fever," the Bee Gees and everything disco. I had graduated early from high school and was on my first flight down to Rio de Janeiro, feeling great wearing my fashionable polyester clothes. I planned on experiencing Brazilian life and studying my third foreign language, Portuguese. I met Beth's entire family and realized that they all speak at least four languages each. I was in heaven. I found my second family. Beth and I liked many of the same things as teenagers like music, dance, the outdoors, social events, fashion, languages and travel. Rejane, her mother and a native Brazilian, was a successful international economist who worked for the Brazilian government and traveled the world for her job. Her stepfather, Peter, was a German executive in the perfume industry. Her younger siblings Veronica and Jan were in international private grade schools. I really felt like I belonged here, except for my clothes. My dream life was gradually coming together for my next phase of life and my global education. I had the time of my life in Brazil, practicing all of my languages with the family, experiencing a new culture, new language and new foods.

While in Brazil, I met another California girl. Cherie had a similar path as mine with languages, studies, travel and being the only one in her family who had an interest. We became friends and planned out our next phase together for university studies, languages and travels back in the USA once we left Brazil. My challenge was to get accepted at the University, yet I did it. Cherie and I entered Cal State university Sacramento because of its extensive foreign language and foreign exchange student programs, I actively participated every year and spent part of each year in a different country perfecting my languages and foreign studies. My success and confidence continued to grow.

As my planning and intention-setting would have it, a few years later in 1981, I spent my junior year in college in France with my BFF and her family. Her family had relocated from Brazil to Paris, France. I was planning to study in the south of France at a university in Aix-en-Provence. I set the intention that I could find a university in Paris that would cooperate and collaborate with my university in the USA. I found the American University in Paris and all worked out great. My BFF Beth and I got an apartment together and had the time of our lives living in Paris in our early 20s enjoying food, fashion and flirting with young men. It was fabulous. We were living our dream! We dreamed it, planned it and took all the action steps possible to make it a reality.

Fast forward a few years later to 1985...I learned to incorporate the same strategy of success with my languages and travel into my corporate life as a working professional. I envisioned in my mind what the next stage of my life would look like, then set out a plan of how to achieve it. I was open to receive new possibilities in my career life and I had exceptional success. I was getting promoted left and right and relocating to different offices with new responsibilities in the insurance industry. It's where I met my spouse of 28 years.

I've inspired my spouse and so many other connections to go travel and explore the world. Sometimes this started off by visiting an international cuisine restaurant. I'd paint the vision and inspire them with some of my experiences. Not knowingly at the time, I had inspired many of my relatives to become host families. It seemed like the 1990s/early 2000s was an era where many families were becoming very global. Several nieces and nephews studied and lived abroad. Several other relatives had interests in traveling abroad, too. My husband and I hosted another student. We were giving back, yet I wanted to give back in an even bigger way.

I have a deep-rooted sense of giving back and contributing to our world in deeds, such as helping students. I and others have helped raise money for the Boys & Girls Club of America, helped build bottle schools in Guatemala (where I was fortunate enough to reconnect with a family I lived with decades prior) and helped foreign students in their transition to study abroad programs by working as a representative of Foreign Exchange Programs and hosting additional students. It's been an amazing adventure.

I met an emotional challenge when I received a devastating phone call one Sunday night, a week before Easter in 2004. My Brazilian mother, Rejane, rang to tell me my BFF Beth was dying of cancer and the end was near. It was time to speak with Beth to say my farewells. We spoke and promised that I would be there within the week. Thankfully, my spouse and I vacationed with her in Brazil two years before; she seemed fine, out of remission and doing well, but the cancer spread from her breasts to her spine, head/brain and liver. Somehow, I just intuitively knew when the phone had rung after months of no responses to my emails that it was not good. So, several days before Easter, I arranged time off work and flew from Los Angeles to Sao Paulo, Brazil to be with my Brazilian family.

While I was in Brazil, we were all heartbroken knowing Beth would pass away soon. Beth was in hospice, monitored at home and had gone blind. Thankfully, she was alert enough for a few days to enjoy my company. We shared stories and laughed to ease the tension in the house. Yet, Easter Sunday, she went into the hospital again. It was heartbreaking for us all. Rejane cried for the eventual loss of her first daughter. I reminded Rejane that she had another daughter, Lynn, in the USA. I told her, "I'm here. I want to help create a legacy for your granddaughters and Beth's nieces who are too young to have really known Beth and her Esprit de Vivre." I vowed to host my Brazilian nieces, the children of Veronica, when they were ready. It was agreed.

My husband and I successfully hosted our two Brazilian nieces in 2009 and 2012, both of whom had enriched experiences here in California. They both learned a little more about their late Aunt Beth from me. We now enjoy sharing our lives on social media and have small chats regularly with all my Brazilian family and other international friends. We are all still connected. Beth's spirit still inspires and lives within me.

After the nieces left, I felt a sense of loss. My challenge was to keep my international travel passion alive. I felt I needed something else and I was longing to travel again and connect with others with similar interests. I was in search of a community, I just did not know how to find it. I was lonely and broken on the inside. I was yearning for something else, and then it appeared – a global travel business/club.

The travel business came at a time when I needed to feel uplifted and inspired. I was going through a difficult time. Yet, opportunities show up for a reason. I'd not really done this before as it was different. And yes, it has its challenges and its rewards. Some of the biggest rewards are seeing people's faces smile and light up when they see affordable exciting destinations that they can check off on their bucket lists, and how they can get more excitement or fulfillment back in life with travel, adventure and new memories. When our parent company announced the possibility of dining out to earn travel dollars at select restaurants, I thought, "Wow, this is bringing back memories of my first inspirations to travel: through foreign food."

During this time, my husband and I met so many amazing new friends from networking and our travel community. Community and connections help feed our passions, inspirations and successes, if you are in the right community. If not, change it!

Where I'm at now, we are able to inspire individuals and families to visualize their dream life and dream vacations. We help students become foreign exchange students, adults to do global projects that positively impact the lives of children, families to host foreign students and most importantly, we are able to show working adults it is possible to travel and experience the world affordably, one vacation experience at a time.

Find out what inspires you in life. We all have something that stands out. I really encourage others to dig deep inside on your journey in life and explore what excites you to keep going. Can you visualize that future self? What are you doing? Where are you? What's your environment like? Who is with you? What are your senses picking up? Are you happy? If not, then stop! Re-visualize your future to make sure you are doing activities that bring you joy.

Perhaps, create a vision map/board. Put images on the board that inspire your future life, family, friends, influencers, career, sense of being and sense of abundance.

The first year I did a vision board, I successfully accomplished 75% of what I put on that board. By having a visual reminder, it becomes an indirect accountability for your goals. I took this one step further by itemizing my specific plan for that year, and attached it to the back of my vision board, something I learned from my Feng Shui mentor, Dr. Janet Woods. For those who prefer, create a digital vision board with PowerPoint and Google images (I've been doing this for nearly a decade). You can move the images around and update it at random.

Create a bucket list of things to do and accomplish. See if you can make a list greater than 50; get creative. Have fun with it; go do/be some of it and watch your confidence increase. You'll gain success, confidence and followers.

Do you surround yourself with others who will lift you up? Consider getting into a mastermind group or some type of club/community (or create one). Find someone to hold you accountable to your goals/vision. I've told others some of my big new goals and asked them to ask how I'm progressing each time they see me; it works. I've told people I plan to run a ½ marathon when I never ran even a 5K before! I had a goal of a slimmer/fitter me. I told a lot of people and they watched me successfully and confidently get fit and slim down, which in part, is how I got invited to co-author and publish my first book!

Sometimes, we never know who it is we might inspire in life, yet, if we don't share ourselves and our journeys, how can we expect that result? Did you catch that? Not everyone we inspire in life will tell us directly! That's okay! Go share yourself and successes anyway.

Go out in life and live to the fullest. Do something new. Challenge yourself and watch your confidence grow. Go see the world; there is so much to explore, foods to taste, people to meet and places to see or experience. Go beyond your own borders. Learn something new about other places or people. Share yourself and embrace others and their individuality instead of judging them. LIVE a life that others can not or will not. Become "That Person" and drop the ego. What others think about you or your life is their concern, not yours. Others are not living your life, walking in your footsteps or being the inspirer of life that you are. Go be it. Be the successful, confident and inspiring person you were meant to be.

LYNN'S TIPS & TOOLS

Dream/Visualize what you want that ignites your senses. Summarize your dreams on paper or record it. Organize, plan or map out your life in words in detail.

Create a vision board or map with images that inspire you that mirror your written plan. You can use magazines, PowerPoint or Google images. Put in on your wall or save it as a screen saver.

Get into a community of like-minded others who inspire you. Meet up, look up events on Facebook, Google it or create it. We all need others to encourage us.

Take action. Don't worry about it being perfect. When I first started speaking different languages, my grammar and accents were horrible, yet, I applied what I knew at the time and progressed. The same thing goes with running my first ½ marathon. It takes time and practice.

Track your progress/success over time. This will build your confidence.

Share your journey and inspire others.

Lynn Heubach is an accomplished linguist, foreign traveler, author, travel & retreat expert, entrepreneur and speaker. She speaks several languages, has lived in numerous countries and traveled to dozens of countries where she cultivated many connections. She shares how to go from dreaming to being. Her successes in her travel life and careers in banking, insurance risk management, real estate investing and travel give her a unique perspective on how to achieve greater things in life. She has a compassionate collaborative spirit she combines with goal-setting that helps transcend into remarkable results.

Connect with Lynn
www.TraveLynn2.com • IG @IamTraveLynn2

Live an
INSPIRED
LIFE
filled with

Creativity!

~ Susie Augustin

YOGA – THE KEY TO UNLOCKING THE LIGHT IN ME

by Lola Salazar

When I first saw the Facebook advertisement for Yoga Teacher Training I was like...This is so cool! I want to do this. I had barely taken a handful of classes prior to sign up. After meeting my fellow yogis in training I thought, this will be interesting. I could never even dream the bond I would truly form with these individuals. The teachers told us we would go deep. "Well," I said (in my head of course), "You just try and open me up... Not. Gonna. Happen sister!"

As the weeks progressed and we went deeper into the practice, learning sutras, asanas, different types of yoga and yogic beliefs, I saw my fellow students embracing the flow and getting deep. Each opening up like beautiful sunflowers. Growing and becoming stronger for it. I still looked around at these beautiful enlightened beings, not knowing why I was holding myself back. Yes, I was the loudest. Yes, I was the first one to talk about what's going on and over-sharing life. Did I mention I blabber on, especially when nervous? But all of my past hurts, fears, tears, insecurities were held locked away behind a door. Seeing the courage of my fellow yogis made me believe, when I was ready, that this was a safe space.

It was Chakra day, the day my door unlocked, and some of the darkness behind it pushed through. As I threw my emotional tantrum, as I like to refer to it, the darkness turned to light. I was able to express some of the pent up hurt with humans I trusted. That was empowering. Seeing them not pity me, but feel as I felt. To encourage me that I really am amazing, not 'a person that no one wants to be around'. They didn't know what I had gone through. We all have stories and they all shape us, good and bad.

My stories were painful to face. Growing up I was a loner. I struggled with friendships and how to fit in. Things went from bad – all the girls in my 6th grade class getting up and leaving the lunch table as soon as I sat down. To worse – having to do home schooling because of the extreme stress and anxiety I would feel, especially after being kicked out of another group and told no one wants you here. My self-esteem was horrible and the self-talk was worse. I began to self-inflict pain, battle anxiety, depression and suicidal thoughts. I never really fit in during my younger years. I know looking back I tried too hard. I was annoying and clingy. I just wanted to be accepted by my peers. I had a great home life with parents that cared and did everything and anything they could, and my grandparents lived three houses down the street. I had a little sister I adored and enjoyed being with all the time. Life was good by all means, but I just couldn't figure out why I was the way I am. Why did it stress me out to be in social situations where I had to converse? I was terrified to go in public or hang out with people I didn't know. If it wasn't for my best friend, Jen, in high school I would have never known that I could actually be accepted for the chubby weird creature I was.

I married at 18 and even though we cared and loved each other, we were just a toxic mess. After nearly eight years of a bad roller coaster relationship we finally ended things. It came the year after we had our amazing little warrior son, Cordova.

I moved back in with my parents and went a little wild. After the birth of my little valkyrie Pandora, we had Cordova tested and found him to be on the autism spectrum. I had to get my shizz together, I now had two kids needing me at my best. My parents are personal development nuts, my sister and I grew up listening to them go on and on about how wonderful PD was. I always thought it was interesting and great...for them. But struggled with it myself. After being surrounded by it again, with my parents graciously taking my broke single mom self to these seminars, I slowly started to open up. My mom would take me to women's retreats and I would be encompassed by all these beautiful souls that were shockingly kind to each other, and they were ALL woman! I went from zero self-esteem to pretty much giving little effs about what others think, and it reflects in my appearance and personality. Now don't get me wrong, it is still a struggle some days. Now though, I don't let my fears hold me back like they would have before.

Starting yoga was my journey to my freedom from self. I have changed and evolved. Two years ago I wouldn't have been able to be open and raw on this public of a level. Now I'm able to stand in front of a class of people and instruct them how to move their bodies. By teaching yoga to others I find that it is the best place to grow internally as well as externally. I share with my students that it is not a competition. That yoga is your own personal practice. Use it as you see fit. I work mostly with beginners. The reward I have of seeing my students successfully nail asanas that they were not sure of when I first taught them is just so encouraging.

On my first day of Yoga Teacher Training, our teachers asked, why are you doing yoga? My response was for health – both physical and mental. I am such a believer in natural healing. I want to help others feel their best, from the inside out. I'm excited to be in a nutrition program, learning more to be of better service to my yogis.

LOLA'S LIFE HACKS

🎙 Yoga – Take a private class...it's a game changer.

🎙 Yoga – Props are your friends, never ditch your friends.

🎙 Yoga – It's never a comparison. 98% of the time the person on the mat next to you doesn't even know you exist. They are trying to get in the same pose as you. Ain't no one got time to look around and judge.

🎙 Life – Never stop dreaming.

🎙 Life – Letting my kids be who they want to be (dress, talk, interests, etc.) has helped me be who I want to be.

🎙 Life – No matter what or who, be true to you.

Lola Salazar is a mom to two awesome kiddos. She believes in family first. She has the greatest support of her family, her 'sister from another mister' and her long-term boyfriend Efren. Her favorite pastimes are going to the gym, yoga, hanging out at her parents' house, reading, or spending time with her kids and family or close friends. She also loves to travel. She looks to open her practice further by taking classes for children with special needs, seniors as well as anything else that strikes her fancy. Her family has 2 rescue dogs and 1 crazy kitty. Lola's dream is to work remotely and travel the world with her kids and loved ones. What's your dream?

Connect with Lola
IG @LunaLolaYoga

LIVING STRONG

by Shawna "Strong" Pierce

Whoa, she's muscular. That's what most people think when they see me. I am a female bodybuilder, which is not quite considered as falling into the category of "feminine" to most of the world. It is a lifestyle requiring attributes such as discipline, motivation, perseverance, planning and preparation to achieve this physique. The focus becomes about eating, sleeping, cooking, and training daily. Every day involves evaluating and feeling for progress. To be successful as a professional bodybuilder, there is no slacking off, and even on lazy days you still must go to the gym.

Sporting this body around means I receive a lot of looks, and of course, judgements. So, I was not just in the competitive scene on stage, but also on the stage of society. Here is where I found who I was and was not. I never really tried to fit in anywhere, because I did not really belong to any category. I realized over time it isn't important to fit into anything. There is no reason to conform to societal expectations or to accept the beliefs and ideals of others. What worked for me, is what felt right to me and this is what gave me peace of mind.

My life has always led up to wanting to be a Superwoman. This does not just mean to be in ultimate physical condition, but to be the best woman I can be, period. To become this means exercising healthy thoughts and behaviors that are conducive to growth. This includes (but is not limited to), understanding my values, having good intentions, maintaining my inner truth, and building honesty and trust with myself and others. These things take constant nurturing. Being this way is a discipline, especially today when we have so much around us to manipulate and divert our attention.

The insight that bodybuilding gave me is that I will never reach perfection. Why? Because as long as I compete against others I will never be good enough. There will always be someone who will look better and train harder. What I needed to build upon was my attitude toward myself and life. Without our mental aspects our bodies wouldn't matter. Evolving the depth of who we truly are is not an easy task. Shutting out the ugliness is hard, both around us and inward.

I began to own my power after understanding more about where my attention goes and how my thoughts create my reality. I immersed myself in different cultures (outside of America's bubble) and explored the unknown without letting fear or predisposed beliefs get in my way. This enabled me to turn my attention to questions that really mattered; how much more can I grow and how much more can I experience?

Here is one thing that is important to keep in perspective. Our inner guidance system holds the answers that we often ignore. Intuition is a built-in tool to let us know when we are, or are not, following what feels good. You have to know how you want to feel in order to get where you want to go. You can't find success in anything you do without following your inner compass.

The formula is to find balance in everything we do, think and feel. Self-growth is our pilot in life. Without this we remain the same. Thinking the same merry-go-round thoughts and moving through life in a trance is not a pathway to growth. Fear and worry should never dictate our decisions; they are anchors. Life is supposed to be a trip, so learn to let go.

I challenge you to take yourself to the next level just like I did. Build up your mind, your body, and feed your soul. Exercise, travel, find something new to learn, meditate and take chances. Just don't limit yourself to what your current reality is, because it's changeable. The key word here is expansion. This is how momentum is created and new desires manifest.

I am passionate about empowerment through awareness, and as part of this collective consciousness that we all share, my desire is to help others become their best selves. By addressing your *whole* self, your superhero qualities will emerge and you will feel limitless.

SHAWNA'S INSPIRATION TIPS

Who is your biggest inspiration in life, and what qualities does he or she possess that drew your attention? Write down what qualities you have that you admire. What are your strengths and what things would you want to work on getting better at? This will give you insight on what self-growth tactics you need to work on first.

What is one thing you tell yourself you should be doing that you are putting off? Without making excuses, create a solution. Make a plan to make it happen, and if you can't hold yourself accountable, find someone or an online platform that can (like Stikk.com).

Journal any negative thoughts you have about yourself. Then next to each thought, think about how you can turn it around into a positive one, writing it down. Evaluate the contrast. Over time, you will get better at choosing your words/thoughts and faster at catching yourself.

Visualize yourself completing a project or achieving a goal. Capture the feeling of enjoying the moment. This method plays an important role in making your dreams come to life.

Shawna "Strong" Pierce is a transformational life coach who gives guidance on overall health and well-being. She is a world traveler and an avid seeker of knowledge, wisdom and self-development. Shawna's passion for spreading empowerment led her to her passion for writing about it. Shawna is certified in Neuro-Linguistic Programming, is an IFBB Professional Bodybuilder, and inspirational speaker. She also has a B.S. in Community Health Education as well as in Nutrition, and is a proud U.S. Air Force Veteran.

Connect with Shawna
www.ShawnaStrong.com • Twitter @Bodysculptoraz • IG @ShawnaStrong

THE BLUE SATIN SLIPPERS

by Bonnie Gruttadauria

The smooth, cool fabric hugs my toes as I slide into the delicate, ice-blue slippers. Like Cinderella's glass slippers, they fit perfectly.

The charming fairytale character wished for a handsome prince to sweep her off her feet. Instead, I longed for an embrace from the only person who wore the high-heeled slippers with the blue bows before me – my mother. It took me some time before I realized that my happily-ever-after storybook ending will only come to pass when we are reunited in heaven.

I was 15 years old when my mother died, and the memories I have of her are from the distorted lenses of a child's perspective. Mother/daughter relationships can be difficult, especially during the teenage years, and that's the way it was with the two of us. These days, when I close my eyes I choose to envision my mother mesmerized by the music of her favorite song, Glenn Miller's "Moonlight Serenade," dancing in her dainty slippers as if floating on air without a care in the world. This ethereal vision of my mother –happy, free and giddy with life— is quite different from the stern, frugal, no-nonsense parent I remember. Sadly, near the end of her life, I watched her spirit fade as she became pain-ridden and frail before succumbing to colon cancer. Peering through the hazy gossamer curtain of time makes reconciling the real and imaginary images challenging.

The slippers are fashioned from luxurious satin. Perhaps my mother bought them on impulse or before practicality became an issue...dominating her wardrobe and her thinking. They are certainly more frivolous than other footwear I saw my mother purchase for herself or for me. Her closet contained a minimal assortment of sensible pumps. The basic Buster Brown tie-up shoes she bought for me as a young girl were often strewn on my bedroom floor. I grin wryly at the memory of my ice skates that were purchased two sizes too big because she insisted I would grow into them.

Questions arise as I try to make a connection with the mother who died much younger than the age I am today. Did she feel light on her feet as she twirled to the music of the night? Did she buy the slippers when she was in a romantic frame of mind to delight my father, or did she simply acquire the pretty pair as a gift to herself? Would she scold me or smile if she caught me trying them on decades later? What a joy it would be to have a conversation with her now that I am an adult! I wonder what it would be like to learn and understand her deepest thoughts and passions. Would she be proud of me? Dare I dream of ever filling her shoes?

After my mother's death, my father kept his wife's memory so close to his heart that he was unwilling or perhaps unable to share his love for her with me. I feared that if I mentioned her name, his emotional bandages would unravel and expose raw wounds that never healed.

I visit the cemetery where my mother is buried as a gesture of respect but find little comfort where others experience tranquility. I feel closest to her when I open the lid of the tattered shoe box with the faded department store label and gently remove the blue satin slippers from the yellowing tissue paper. I let my fingers glide down the smooth vamp and across the open toe of each of the slippers. The shape of my mother's feet are still imbedded on the cushioned soles. By touching them, I feel the undeniable imprint of her love on my soul, and I am at peace.

BONNIE'S INSPIRATION TIPS

- Put Yourself in Another Person's Shoes – No one truly knows what issues others are dealing with unless they tell you. Be kind, compassionate and supportive.

- Build the Bridge over Troubled Waters – If it's a struggle to communicate with someone, find what you have in common, share new positive experiences and build on the relationship from there.

- Accept People for Who They Are – Then make peace with it. You can only control your own behavior, so choose positivity.

- Search for the Silver Lining – In a difficult situation, there is always a ray of light. Find the bright spot; let it warm your heart and melt your hard edges.

- Strive to Live Your Best Life – The greatest honor you can give a loved one is to live your own authentic life and be your true self. Be brave, vulnerable and embrace life with gratitude.

- Have a Sense of Humor – Laughter is still the best medicine and greatly reduces your stress level.

 **Bonnie Gruttadauria** is a published author, editor, journalist, news-correspondent, columnist, blogger, public speaker, communications expert, photographer and model. Her work has been featured in *MD Magazine, The News-Herald*, Arhaus Furniture advertisements, Visit Huntington Beach/Surf City USA® blogs and on KTLA-TV. She also received top honors for photography and writing from the National School Public Relations Association. Bonnie's professional fashion and runway modeling credits include Bride World, Catan Fashions, IMTA (International Models and Talent) and John Robert Powers Talent and Modeling Agency.

Connect with Bonnie
FB Tools & Tips for Baby Boomer Chicks
Linkedin.com/in/Bonnie-Gruttadauria-69039212/

Cherish
your dreams,
as they are telling your
HEART
THE TRUTH.

~ Kim Somers Egelsee

FROM AWFUL TO AWESOME: SHIFT YOUR LIFE

by Anush Hovsepyan Gagua

Dear friend, if you are reading this, it means that you, just like me, have also been on a journey of moving from awful to awesome+ , and are always looking for ways to better your life, yes? Before you read any further ask yourself, "Where exactly am I emotionally in my life, most of the time?"

Do I feel awful?

Do I feel OK?

Do I feel good?

Do I feel great?

Do I feel awesome+?

Wherever you are in life, be honest with yourself. There is a reason why I am called to share my journey with you. The reason is not to boast how awesome my life is now, but to openly share how was I able to shift my life up as much as I can in a few pages. On this journey I got to study and apply tools/techniques in personal and professional development that allowed me to handle anything that life threw at me, without being stuck in the "awfulness" of it all and move up to what I truly wanted. So can you.

Eleven years ago, with tears on my face, I was fueling my black Jetta VW in Glendale, CA with the last quarters I had saved for my laundry. I felt awful inside out. There I was alone in Los Angeles, no job, no money for next month's rent, no money for food... even though that very evening I was invited to a board meeting in a mansion in Glendale Hills to discuss a big concert project with Stevie Wonder and Chaka Khan, by people who I wasn't aligned with. That very morning my roommate at the time (whom I had allowed to live with me rent-free for a while), had told me that she wouldn't be able to wait until my crisis was over, and she moved in with another friend. So, in a way, I was also feeling awfully betrayed. Oh, and I found out the guy that I used to date was using cocaine. So I had broken up with him, as well. As if all of that was not awful enough, I had these married, old, affluent men hitting on me. What?! How disgusting.

How did I get here? I was consuming more than creating, and hence I was consumed in all aspects of my life. Simple cause and effect... I had surrounded myself mostly with people who were toxic and only were takers. I was consuming every penny I was making. In short, I was giving all my time and energy to projects and people that I was not aligned with, except a TV show that I was hosting at that time. The TV show was my outlet/bubble where I felt the happiest by interviewing renowned people on their path to success, and with that, living in the illusion that their lives were somewhat mine. You probably guessed, I was also living paycheck to paycheck. Unfortunately, the TV station that I was working for (owned and run by people with a heart of gold with no business skills needed to bring in the actual gold needed) went bankrupt. I had no idea. I found out the hard way. I kept getting phone calls from people that knew me, saying that my show and the channel it was on was off the air. I called the owners. They said they didn't want to tell me earlier, but Charter Communications had taken away the channel from them due to inability to pay the broadcast fees. What was I going to do? This meant no more paycheck...no rent, no food. Crisis. It's in times of crisis though, that you get clear about your values. Crisis is an amazing filter for letting go of fluff and anything that is out of alignment and toxic. So, if you are experiencing a crisis, you will see the perfection of it later.

Back to my story. So, after fueling my car with my last quarters, I called a friend who had a house in Studio City and asked if I could stay there for a little while until I figured things out. He said yes. I could stay in his 7-year-old son's room. On days the little boy was visiting, I would sleep on the couch. So, it was in this friend's house that I had the awakening, and started regaining my strength back. My friend stopped me before I was off to my next unpaid board meeting, saying, "Anush, what are you doing? You can't volunteer your time and energy when you have no money for food and shelter. Shift your life." It hit me then. For things to change, I had to change.

In my friend's library I found Tony Robbins's Life Coaching CDs. I read Jack Canfield's Success Principles books. I discovered the world of transformation. I had a folder (I still have it to this day) with "SHIFT YOUR LIFE" written on it, where I highlighted the insight and distinctions from these books and applied it to my daily life. I also took advantage of a free coaching session offered with the CDs. Then I maxed out my credit card and got myself a coach, and went to Unleash the Power Within event. I started each morning strong by doing Power Walks & Talks (you can download these from my website to get you started, as my gift to you). I started being very intentional of my time and big why. I also became very conscious of my environment, the people, the places, the situations I was in and did a big cleanse/detox. I started believing in my values and kept my integrity even when others wouldn't, and some people dropped. There were times where I felt awfully alone because I started turning down invitations and stopped seeing people because I realized they were absolutely out of alignment of what mattered to me at my heart. I learned to be comfortable with the uncomfortable. I learned to sit with the problem until I found a solution. I learned to live my life according to my own standards. In the mornings, when I was having difficulty waking up to another day of uncertainty, I heard Jim Rohn's words, "If you want to have an above average life, you've got to have above average standards." I started meditating and praying. I did the inner work and learned to say no to instant and immediate pleasures because I was drawn by my vision of what I actually want to create, have, do and be in my life. I went into my cocoon to be able to fly like a butterfly.

With the help of coaching, I gradually moved myself up from awful to OK, from OK to Good, from Good to Great, from Great to Awesome, and now I am working on Awesome+ (aka outstanding life). So can you.

Fast-forward nine months later from that day at the gas station. I landed a PR gig for a multimillion dollar company heading their LA operations. l was able to not only rent a place, but I bought a place in LA. I also did a complete Life Detox, letting go of people places, patterns that were not aligned with my values and goals for life.

As my first coach helped me get back on my feet, I was thrilled to discover the profession of coaching. I realized that coaching is my true calling. So, I got my ICF coaching certification, and in addition to my PR practice, I started building up my coaching practice. I named my coaching practice Outstanding Life Coach, as an outstanding life to me meant a life beyond awesome, where you live life on your terms, in your gifts, in alignment with your core values, where you have become more of you vs. pretending to be someone you are not. You are in service and on purpose. My Outstanding Life Coach practice was designed to help people create success plus happiness, by bringing results, joy and mastery in their lives. I started helping people achieve more with less stress, working specifically with clients intending to make major transitions and leaps in their personal or professional lives.

Soon enough, I got my coaching niche: extremely hardworking, high-achiever, multi-talented individuals with big goals and a big heart, struggling with saying "no" and taking on too much. I guess I ended up coaching clients like me. To coach successfully you've got to be a few steps ahead of the path of your coachee. And, of course, what makes the coaching relationship effective and unlike any other relationship, is that as a coach you have evidence based tools, techniques and the training to help bouncing back and climbing high easier and faster. To this day, I have a coach myself. And life still challenges me with awful situations/events, yet what I know for certain is that life cannot be awesome in all aspects of your life all the time. What's different now is that I acknowledge what's awful, and then using my toolbox, I am able to get out of it faster and go further. I coach my clients to do the same, I am here to ensure you that you too can shift and better up your life.

It is so inspiring to see my coaching clients own their strengths and bloom, as they get life-changing results, such as getting admitted to med school or law school, increasing team productivity and engagement, getting represented by Hollywood's top acting agency, moving out of a toxic relationship, getting promoted, moving to sunny California and more.

So my question to you is this... If you had a magic wand (we don't, but we'll imagine we do), what is one goal in your life that if you made that happen, everything else will be so much better? Write that down as this vision has the power to pull you up and better you up every single day when the going get's tough.

It is amazing to see people go so much farther, faster with a strong vision and the power of coaching. In the Olympics the best players have coaches. Even the CEO of Google, Eric Schmidt, has a coach. Ever wonder why? Because a great coach helps you do your best, helps to discover your strengths even when the going gets tough. A great coach helps to not only get the results you're after, but to also enjoy your achievements. As a great believer in coaching, I am honored to coach amazing people to achieve their career and life goals. To give you an example of transformation, my coaching client, celebrity Hanna Griffiths, has agreed to share her coaching experience to inspire others in her shoes. She started coaching with me, after being dropped by a very powerful agent. Just like me when I started my coaching, she was quite successful to the outside world, as she was in major TV and print campaigns with billboards on Sunset Blvd in Los Angeles, yet she was burned out. She had given her power to others. After several weekly coaching sessions, she started to take ownership of her own strengths and abilities to make things happen even without her powerful agent backing her up. Through coaching we brought her time/energy/focus to what is within her control and influence, vs. on what she can't control or influence. Most importantly she had the awakening that otherwise her livelihood and dreams were at stake. And, just like my transformation, here is what happened to my coaching client Hanna.

"When I first started working with Anush, I knew exactly what I wanted but I didn't know how I was going to get it. And I was working so hard but was often frustrated. Anush shifted my perspective on things; she guided me to take actions/ choices that would benefit me in the long run. Focusing on my big game allowed me to free up and not let insignificant things affect me. In just 6 months of working with her weekly, I have doubled my monthly earnings, started working with an Oscar winning director, signed with a top talent management company and a top talent agency. Coaching with Anush has been one of the most important influences in my life. She is my secret to success." ~ Hanna Griffiths, Actress/Producer

You may say, but I don't want to be a Hollywood star, I am just a working mom trying to balance everything. To me motherhood, or giving birth to any result/project that can be life-changing is equally powerful as making it in Hollywood. As a mother, I love coaching working moms as they expand their identity and need to balance work and life with this precious life-changing baby. There is nothing as difficult, yet as rewarding and meaningful as motherhood. As I help shape my daughter Gina's model of the world, the way she makes sense of this world, the way she is conditioned, the way she goes back into the game after falling, I realize that motherhood is the best coaching opportunity every day and every minute, literally and metaphorically.

Wherever you are in life, I honor you. Do your share with the tips, tools and resources I came to master throughout the years, make daily shifts and pretty soon you will move up and see immediate positive changes in your life. I invite you to visit my website for the coaching programs and workshops I run. Also, download my Power Walk soundtrack that I have created for you to start shifting your life.

ANUSH'S "7 SHIFTS UP" TIPS

Wherever you are in life, be honest with yourself. Face the truth. Don't avoid or numb it.

Create a compelling vision of your future. Be clear of what you truly want at your core.

Be clear about your why and your values. What is important to you if time and money were not an issue? Live in your values.

Detox and upgrade your environment, including your body, your friends and network. Keep only what/ whoever supports your values and goals.

Take massive action toward your outcomes.

Measure your progress not your problems.

Celebrate your achievements and progress before you jump into what's next.

Anush Gagua is an ICF certified Business and Life Results Coach/Speaker, creating results in clients' lives with renewed sense of purpose, confidence and drive. She helps individuals and teams achieve more with less stress. Clients include celebrities, as well professional teams such as Wyndham Hotels, ABHES, LA Chambers of Commerce and more. In 2019 Anush joined BetterUp's Global Network of Expert Coaches. She's is a former PR executive & CNN World Reporter with 15+ years combined experience. She holds a Masters Degree from UNC-Chapel Hill, and has graduated from Coachville and several Tony Robbins programs. Anush is mothering a beautiful 5-year-old girl, Gina, in sunny California.

Connect with Coach Anush
www.OutstandingLifeCoach.com

CARPE DIEM

Mark Twain said, "Life is short, break the rules, forgive quickly, kiss slowly, love truly, laugh uncontrollably, and never regret anything that made you smile ... Explore. Dream. Discover." This is carpe diem, "seize the day." Make the most of each day, each minute, your whole life. It is taking the time to travel, go to concerts, hug your friends, dance in the kitchen and wear the red dress. It is learning to filter out caring what people think; who are "they" anyway? It is becoming comfortable in your own skin, confident with your choices and conscious about what you really desire and how you want to feel. This allows you to jump into amazing sudden opportunities when they're presented to you.

Today matters! Don't get so stuck in the regrets of yesterday, or anxiety of tomorrow. Do you love your job, or are you in a rut – living a life of "have-to's"? Get off the "hamster wheel" of life. One way to do this is having passion for life. What are you passionate about? Do you take time for your hobbies? Living a life you love also opens you up to opportunities: of love, success and more. Dare to live the life of your dreams and embrace each day.

Having the philosophy, mantra and attitude of carpe diem can change your life, help you find the good, the gratitude and the gifts in each moment. Carpe Diem.

A RAY OF SUNSHINE

by Janet Norraik

Coming to America from a Latin country where the only popular sport was soccer, it *never* crossed my mind that one day I was going to become a "Hockey Mom". I grew up in a small town where ice hockey was never even mentioned! The very first time my face appeared on television, I was in the sidelines rooting for my son. The viewers described me as a "ray of sunshine!"

Ever since I was a child, I've had this effect on people. I remember walking to the river and holding my grandma's hand while listening to her love stories and life adventures. My grandmother played the biggest role in my life because she taught me to believe in a higher power and not to fear. I thank her every day for that because during the hard times, I've always been able to stay strong and keep my faith. I think of Abuelita every day because thanks to her, I learned to love myself and to always see the good in others.

When I was a teenager, I started a new chapter in life and moved to California. This was around the same time that I met my soulmate and "mi amor" in Los Angeles. He moved from Boston the same year that I came to the states and we have been happily married for over two decades. Once we were married and got pregnant with our son, my husband's pure joy at finding out the news was overwhelming. He bought a puck and a hockey stick, hoping and staying optimistic that our son would have the gift to be able to play the game of hockey. My son Geno came into this world on December 28,1998, and brought a love into my heart that I had never before experienced. Always my son, forever my friend. And wouldn't you know it, he became an incredible hockey player!

It's been so surreal living the amazing, fun and extraordinary world as proud hockey parents. We have built priceless memories that will last a lifetime, including bonding with my son's teammates and their parents. Even to this day, people always doubt me or question me whenever I use the title "Hockey Mom." I'll always hear, "How is this possible?" or "No offense, but you are Hispanic." In other words, because of my looks and strong accent, there was no way I could possibly be in the hockey world – at least according to them. Every time my son Geno won a hockey tournament, I would always wear his winning big medal for a whole month at work and would announce to the whole world how proud I was of my son's team. His room is full of trophies, hat trick pins and medals of all sizes, including the one MVP Geno received in Canada in 2013.

The highest points of my life all include watching my son hit the ice rink, looking on in awe at the passion he exudes while playing the game he loves. I had a tradition to ask my son to score a goal for his mom a few minutes before every game, and even today I'm always the one screaming the loudest and dancing to the background music. I love every second and I am his biggest fan! Hockey has taught my family the importance of dedication, discipline and leadership.

Geno first started skating at the age of three, and by the time he was five, he was suiting up in full gear and playing games as a forward. He began playing travel hockey at age six and has been playing hockey in rinks all around the country and Europe ever since. One of my most memorable and exciting moments was when Geno scored the game winning goal at the 2011 National Championship. Geno is now 20 years old and continues to play college hockey as a forward at Cal State University Northridge. He just received a certificate of recognition for outstanding academic achievement in Business and Economics, earning him a place on the Dean's List. Geno has a very bright and successful future ahead of him. Looking back on my grandmother's lessons, I too have encouraged my son to always put God first! He lived his life with the thought that success is the ability to give back to others.

I am strong, independent, motivated, hard working, reliable, loyal, determined, selfless, dedicated, loving, compassionate and very funny. *I'm a Hockey Mom.* I'm a magnet to positive energy and good vibes! Put simply, I am a ray of sunshine.

JANET'S LIFE LESSONS

- Living, loving and laughing through life is a must if you want to live to your full potential. Don't be afraid to spice up your life - do crazy things because life is too short to not live "la vida loca!" And of course, spend time with people who make you laugh!

- F.L.Y. – First Love Yourself because when you follow this amazing inner feeling, everything else will fall into line. In order to have a healthy and happy relationship with anyone in your life, you must love yourself first.

- Try new things! Have no fear and get out of your comfort zone. Take risks and don't be afraid to fail or get rejected, because this is how you become stronger.

- Sing and dance every day! This will keep you young, and singing will help you deal with the traffic when commuting to work. Dance is a great form of exercise, and working out will help shape your female curves that keep you looking fit and sexy.

- Tell your loved ones how much you love them every day! Do not take anyone for granted; remind them how grateful you are for them. Be a ray of sunshine wherever you go and fill people with happiness.

- See more of the world if you can. Take family vacations because memories are what life is all about. Say no to material things and put your family first; it's the little things in life that will make you happy.

- In order to succeed, start by doing what's necessary, then by doing what's possible, and suddenly, you are doing the impossible!

JANET'S INSPIRATION TIPS

🎙️ Always put God first! If you feel any pressure in life, it means that God is bringing the best out of you. Amen!

🎙️ We were born to be real, not to be perfect. Learn to love your imperfections. Perfection can be boring. It's all about *chemistry* not anatomy.

🎙️ Do not pay attention to your age. Feel like a very expensive bottle of wine, the older the better!

🎙️ Act like you own the world because you do. Enjoy the freedom to do the things that make you happy. It's all up to you.

🎙️ Love your parents. Keep in mind they are getting older. Be the reason why your parents have a smile today.

🎙️ Dreams require action, but don't have expiration dates.

 **Janet Norraik** was born in Central America. She took classes in theater and music, and was passionate about singing and performing, learning to play the piano at age ten. She's been a certified medical assistant for 30 years. Her expertise is in facial, plastic and reconstructive surgery and dermatology, sterile techniques and sales. Janet appeared in the television show on the very popular "E" TV show, Botched; she was the medical assistant for Dr. Nassif and Dr. Dubrow. She's a dynamic radio host for a well-known Mexican motivational radio show. She's also Vice President of a non-profit and loves helping others. She is happily married and a proud ice hockey mom to her son Geno who competes at national level.

Connect with Janet
IG @JanetNorraik

From Wall Street To Main Street

by Vance Mizzi

I'm sitting in a large office with degrees on the walls, very nice furniture, a large desk and big plush leather chairs. I'm thinking to myself, "Wow, I must really be someone now." I've never been in the doctor's office, only exam and waiting rooms. But today, my doctor made an appointment to see me in his personal office. I think to myself, "This Wall Street thing is really paying off. I don't even have to wait to see him. I must be pretty important these days". He is sitting behind the desk reading the test results that just came in. My wife sent me to see him a few weeks earlier after I passed out climbing the stairs in our home on Long Island. He did not share in my amusement when I showed up for the exam weeks earlier with a note from my wife addressed to him in a sealed envelope.

After a few awkward moments, I break the ice with my very clever line, "What's up doc?" With that, he drops the file on his desk gets up and says, "You know you're going to die if you keep this up, don't you?" At that moment, things got serious and all of a sudden, I realized he did not invite me into his office for small talk and a possible stock tip. He began to read my vitals to me, "You my friend are 5'8" and 265lbs. You have high blood pressure, the onset of diabetes, you drink too much, your wife can't sleep at night because she has to constantly roll you over due to your sleep apnea and you are going bald! If you don't make some BIG changes, and soon, you will not see your 40th birthday! Am I making myself perfectly clear?"

It's now the following Monday at 5:30 am and I am sitting in my office in a Fortune 100 financial planning firm, getting ready to accept a big promotion that will undoubtedly change my and my wife's lives forever. I am about to be the regional Vice President of the Northeast Zone. That's a BIG promotion. I am surrounded by white office boxes that need to be filled with all of my files, awards, photographs and personal belongings. Today, I am negotiating the color of my new car, moving allowances, readying my house for sale and in a few hours, I am going to address my team and give them the news.

My boss walks in and very deadpan says, "Unpack your shit, you're not going anywhere. I'm gonna need you here for a few more years. I called the home office and told them to give your spot to the other guy." At that moment, the walls around me and the windows behind me all seemed to collapse. My well-tailored suit and shirt seemed to get a bit tight in the collar. It was the middle of November in New York and I began to sweat. I thought to myself, "The doctor was right, I am not going to see 40, I am going to have heart attack and die right here behind this corporate desk I've been chained to for the last ten years."

It's 7:30 am and all of my team is showing up, pulling their ties tight and buttoning their suit jackets as they shake off the cold. Another day at the office. I think to myself, "not today" and decide to go have a talk with the boss. I did not get here by laying down and accepting the status quo. I got here by fighting for everything I believed in, bleeding the company colors, outworking the competition, playing the corporate game and today it was my turn to taste victory, today it was my turn to drink from the cup.

As I walked down the long wood paneled hall that separated our two offices, I was reviewing what I was going to say. This was not the first time we disagreed, but we were always able to work things out. His secretary tried to stop me from going in, I walked past her and through the double doors. He got up from his desk as one of the most profanity riddled arguments ensued. After a few minutes passed, I understood this was not going to end the way I planned and those big changes the doctor talked about a few days earlier were about to take place. By now, there was a crowd outside the door and even a few higher ups standing in the room with us. I walked over to his desk, grabbed a yellow post it from his dispenser and with my Mont Blanc pen, I resigned. As I was being escorted from the office by security, an overwhelming sigh of relief came over me. I realized, change was going to do me good. Driving home on the Long Island Expressway, I called my one true friend, my true north, the one person I could count on, my wife. "Hi, honey, it's, me. I just quit my job." Her answer was simple, "Are you OK?" "Yes," I answered, "Actually I am great." "What's the plan?" she asked... and it hit me. I knew I could get another gig, I mean, what just happened was epic and there would be companies that would throw deals at me.

"Let's move to Los Angeles, I will sell real estate and you can open a private practice doing your fitness training and nutrition coaching. It's not going to be easy but let's make some massive shifts in our world starting today." By the grace of God, she agreed right there on the phone, gave her two weeks' notice at the gym she worked at and we landed in California in early February. We found a little place by the beach and started what would be the most epic journey of our lives.

Today, I am nearly 50 years old. By utilizing everything Wall Street taught me, I cold-called my way into the Los Angeles beach city real estate market. I train and mentor over 50 agents and help run a company of nearly 300. I take no medication, I've lost over 110 pounds and my hair grew back! No, seriously, it grew back! My wife is a successful transformational nutrition coach with on-line courses and does in-person sessions as well. I sing and play guitar in a band and we are truly living a fantastic, blessed life.

I have come to realize that sometimes the things we don't expect in life, are our true blessings. It's not what happens to us, it's how we react to those things that truly matters. Life changes in an instant, be ready for it. There is no room for doubt and fear in this world. Faith, sincerity and our passions are where our true success lives. I live everyday grateful for yesterday and enthusiastic about tomorrow. Dream big, dream bold and never let someone tell you how your life is supposed to be. Decide and do everything in your power to make it so. Then and only then will you too live the life of your dreams.

VANCE'S TIPS FOR SUCCESS, CONFIDENCE & INSPIRATION

🎤 Be the person you would most like to be around and learn from.

🎤 Expect to succeed at what you put your mind to...It is failure that should surprise you, never success.

🎤 Think BIG and dream, don't fear failure, pursue success. Focus on what needs to be done and do it.

🎤 Positive self-talk. We already know you are your worst critic, so how about being your biggest supporter? While you're at it...find the positive in others and speak to that, choose your words carefully in your head and be careful of what comes out of your mouth.

🎤 Focus on things you can have an impact on or make changes for the good of others.

🎤 Give back! Donate your time, money, ideas and experience. It is amazing the impact our words and actions have on others.

🎤 Learn from your mistakes, be willing to teach others and never lose faith in what you are doing. You can change course but don't lose faith.

 **Vance Mizzi** is a licensed Realtor and owns a successful Real Estate practice, The Mizzi Group Inc. in the South Bay beach cities of Los Angeles. Born and raised on Long Island, he and his wife moved to California in 2009. He has successfully built his company from the ground and up, he is a a mentor and performance coach in the Real Estate community. He and his wife are fitness buffs and can be seen hiking, kickboxing and doing yoga in local studios around town. A musician since he was 12 years old, he is active in the Los Angeles music scene today.

Connect with Vance
www.theMizziGroup.com • FB The Mizzi Group • IG @VanceMizzi

THE STORIES YOU SHARE WILL IMPACT OTHERS

by Kathy Bair

Encouraging, helping and lifting up others. As a health practitioner, I'm really good at that. But when it came to me, I wasn't so good. I had grown up feeling very insecure about myself in so many ways. I had carried all of that into my adult life and I struggled behind a smile. Then one day in August 2017, there I was in the most out of my comfort zone, bold, crazy moment...standing in the middle of a circular stage speaking to over 20,000 entrepreneurs! The last 24 hours had been a whirlwind!

When I received the message that I was really being asked to do this, it really put me in a spin. Self-doubt crept in. Why would anyone want to hear me? What will I say? Can I do this? OMG! What will I wear? Did the founder of the company really want me on stage sharing business building strategies that I use? All of this ran through my mind as I waivered back and forth for a couple of hours. I reached out to a couple friends and also my incredible mentor. Having a positive support team is so important. They are there for you in many ways. I didn't want too many people to know because if I was going to do this I needed to protect my energy. One friend helped me put together my outfit. Another friend prayed with me and took me through some energy clearing sequences. My mentor infused me with calm and confidence that I could do this and helped me review my talking points. They totally lifted me up.

Did I still have fear? Yes, I did! I was just learning to face fear head on. Fear can paralyze you, but really what is it? It may seem very real. I was thinking of all the things that could go wrong, but who knew if any of that would happen? Identifying the fear and talking about what it really is, and then moving through it, gives you amazing freedom. I knew in my heart if I said no, that I would regret it. I said YES! The fear I felt and the knot in my stomach had almost kept me from this amazing experience. One of my friends says, "Fear is a paper tiger." This is so true! Smash that fear and throw it away!

In the few years prior to this, I had been through some events that had me in very deep places of pain. My life had rather imploded. I was crushed, but I had to keep going for my family and myself. I was really good at "circling the wagons" and keeping things going, but I wasn't letting myself feel the emotions inside. You never know how strong you are until things crumble around you. Yes, I had days I cried, I still have times of tears. I survived, and set out on a path of healing and growth because of an amazing circle of people who supported me. It wasn't easy at times as I peeled back layers of protection and opened up. Saying how I felt and what I really wanted wasn't easy for me. It took work, patience and a village of support. I really learned who was there for me during this time. I am so thankful for each of them.

I learned a lot about myself. The process and feelings of growth can be scary! It is uncharted territory. Pushing through the fear and discomfort is so worth it. I learned the importance of self-care in this process. You can become drained and develop health challenges. Spend some time each day in quiet, calm surroundings. Meditate, journal, reflect, whatever lets you connect to yourself and reset. I have found starting each day with a devotional, prayer and journaling helps me. I also love to get pampered with a massage or mani-pedi too. Fueling and supporting your growth helps you stand as you and the feeling of being who you were meant to be is amazing.

So, back to that stage, in front of those 20,000+ people! My talk was not perfect or exactly as I had planned, but I did it. I came off the stage and it was a blur...my legs felt dead, my feet were suddenly screaming and I backed up into a celebrity guest. One of the stage support team handed me a bottled water and had me sit down. I didn't know whether I wanted to laugh or cry. The adrenaline was nuts! I drank the water, stood up and made my way to my seat. I felt exhausted and energized at the same time. After a bit, I picked up my phone and took a look. I was not prepared – it was blowing up with messages and social media posts. This had never entered my thoughts. The people I had reached, the people who were posting and lifting me up. It was incredible and tears streamed down my face. You just never know who you will have a positive influence on!

I realized over the next few days, weeks and even months, as people reached out to me, that I was on a new path. You never really know how important the stories you tell and experiences you share will impact others. Stepping out of that virtual box not only benefits you, but can also benefit and encourage others as well.

So, whatever your story or path just remember YOU CAN! Dream BIG, stay focused and just DO IT! So much is waiting for you on the other side of your comfort zone. The one comment that I will always remember was one by a friend from college. It reads, "Is that the shy Kathy that I knew in college?" My answer to that is, "No, actually it's a new and improved, still evolving version whose story has just started!"

KATHY'S INSPIRATION TIPS

🎤 Your WHY – your WHY should move you deep inside. It should be something powerful to you. Keep it ever present in your mind.

🎤 Don't Quit – so many people quit right on the edge of success! Remind yourself of your WHY.

🎤 Be Accountable – when you are accountable, growth becomes more steady.

🎤 Positive thoughts – this is so powerful. Try to put all your focus into positives and eliminate the poison of negative thoughts.

🎤 Nutrition and Exercise – there are no fences in your body. We need to support it and give it all the things it needs to function optimally. Mind, Body and Spirit.

Kathy Bair has been a Registered Dental Hygienist for over 30 years. In that time she has learned the true importance of health. She loves supporting others to reach their health goals. This path has taken her to a business bringing nutrigenomic testing and cutting edge support to other healthcare practitioners. Kathy loves being a mom to her 2 boys. In her spare time, she practices yoga, reads, and organizes inspiring trainings for the SoCal area with her business.

Connect with Kathy
IG @Kathy_Bair

Dare to
redesign
your *life*
HOW THE TRUE,
DEEP
AUTHENTIC YOU
knows it is
meant to be.

~ Kim Somers Egelsee

GIVE YOURSELF PERMISSION

by Mike Somers

The third time's a charm. My third career is my true passion and purpose, the most rewarding of all my careers, and where I am able to make the most impact in others' lives. What I learned in my first two careers helped to shape my future, and the success I gained in my current career led to me finding work/life balance and creating huge shifts in the way I work and approach life.

After careers as a letter carrier and as a VHS video rental store owner, I began a new career as a Realtor at the age of 41. I quickly realized I was very good at real estate sales. At that time, our office had 80 real estate agents. In my competitive desire to be successful, I began working outrageously long hours. It was not uncommon for me to arrive at the office by 8:30 am and work until midnight. I quite often did this for seven days a week.

My wife of over 20 years at that time was very understanding. My daughter was about 19 at that time and was busy starting her own adult life. Deep down inside, I felt guilty about not spending enough time with my wife, but my desire to be number one won out. There were times when we had a planned trip that I cancelled because the workload was too great. By my third year as a realtor, I became the company's number one realtor. I liked being the best, but I didn't like who I had become. Through my desire to excel, I had lost life's balance.

Other realtors in my office began to do well and the competition to succeed became even greater. I could not let anyone surpass my production numbers. I worked even more hours, was miserable and out of control. For five consecutive years, I was the office's top realtor. During this time, I began to constantly catch severe colds. I began to have headaches, including migraines. What really scared me was the occurrence of chest pains on a regular basis. After living with these conditions for a substantial period of time, I finally went to see my doctor. He performed numerous tests including an EEG. His conclusion was that I was suffering from an extreme case of stress. He emphasized that if I didn't soon make some changes, I would actually have a heart attack.

It was time to do some soul searching. With the help of my wife and through lots of prayer, I made some necessary decisions. I reduced my workload substantially. I began taking at least one weekend day off every week and got home each night in time for dinner. My production did diminish, but I was still successful. Instead of number one, I was now content to be in the top ten. My life improved in every way. My health improved and I began getting in shape. I lost 50 pounds! I was enjoying life again and my marriage improved.

I have now been a Realtor for 27 years. My workload is substantially lighter by design. I have no plans to retire, as I wish to remain productive. The thing I have finally learned to do is to give myself permission to not work so hard. For a former "workaholic," that was difficult. Currently, I schedule my personal and family events, as well as numerous pleasure trips first, and my work is scheduled around those times. As a further result, my relationships with my family are the best ever. My marriage is now great with November to be our 50th anniversary. I have special close relationships with my daughter and son-in-law. My granddaughters love to spend time with us. Our entire family travels together throughout each year. Last year we went to Lake Tahoe, Italy, and Cabo San Lucas together. This year we will be going to Lake Tahoe again and Hollywood Beach, Florida to bring in 2020 New Year. Life is great when you "give yourself permission."

MIKE'S SUCCESS TIPS

 Work hard and play hard, while maintaining life's balance.

Your level of intensity of work must include time for family, friends, and health maintenance.

The life path you choose must not allow for regrets later in life.

Travel often and enjoy your life and relationships.

Mike Somers is the #1 bestselling author of *Confessions From a Mailman Turned Realtor.* He studied business at CSUN, then became a letter carrier from 1969 to 1984, and served as President of the local branch of the National Association of letter carriers. Later, for seven years Mike and his wife Nancy owned and ran VHS video rental stores called Video Valley. For the past 27 years he has been a Realtor working with Park Regency Realty. He also plans and leads their monthly personal development and success workshops with interviews and speakers. Mike and his wife Nancy have been married nearly 50 years. They have a beautiful daughter Kim Somers Egelsee and two granddaughters. Mike and Nancy love to travel (especially with Kim's family). They reside in the San Fernando Valley, CA.

Connect with Mike
FB Park Regency Real Estate

A CATALYST FOR CHANGE

Jim Rohn said, "Your life does not get better by chance, it gets better by change." A catalyst is someone whose talk, energy, enthusiasm or actions cause others to shift, change or transform. Being a catalyst for change is a powerful purpose, and even a legacy to leave.

This might mean changing a child's life, the course of a friend's direction, deciding to be in a career that inspires, heals or helps others, taking a tragedy and creating a movement out of it, using your own wisdom, abilities or talents to motivate and live by example – or having the knowledge and energy you bring to a situation, place or person allowing powerful changes to happen.

Making the choice to take command over your life is empowering, and when you take action and responsibility, it is freeing. This liberates you to be your true authentic self, opening you up to change and innovative thinking. When you learn from experiences, you create an opportunity to inspire others to come from a place of empowerment, and transform their own lives.

Being innovative and empowered will drive you to make positive change in the world for those who are in need. Sharing your vulnerability helps you to connect in significant ways in order to make a difference. All shame and embarrassment are put aside to bring about awareness and new ways of thinking for positive outcomes. You'll have the courage to change your life, take risks, and create unconventional ways to help others make the choice to take chances.

Start daring to bring fresh ideas, creativity, energy, enthusiasm to what you do, who you're with and where you go. Notice the difference when you intentionally do this. Ignore convention or being like everyone else and step into being a catalyst for change.

FINDING SŌL BALANCE

by Mary Sushinski

What is my life purpose? I have asked myself this question throughout my life, but lately it's been thought consuming. I always thought that purpose equated to success – in my accomplishments, talents, and financial prosperity. Recently some very inspiring women in my life suggested that my purpose doesn't need to be my career. But rather, my gifts of who I am and how I share those gifts with others. At the age of 45 I didn't expect to do a 180 degree turn in my life. I am on a journey of rediscovering myself through physical, mental and spiritual lessons.

"Success isn't just about what you accomplish in your life. It's about what you inspire others to do." ~ Anonymous

Born in 1973, my twin sister Ann and I entered the world only two minutes apart. My mom, a registered nurse, knew something was wrong with me. The hospital staff thought I was fine. Through my mom's persistence, by my third day it was realized that something was terribly wrong. I needed open heart surgery immediately! I was what they called a 'blue baby.' After surgery, it wasn't clear I was going to survive, as the technology and operating on the heart was still a newer concept. My father recalls the moment he knew without a doubt that I was going to make it. On a hospital visit one day he said he saw a vibrant light in my eyes and that was the moment he knew I was going to be OK.

I was OK. I was just like any other kid. Except, for that big zipper scar that ran down my chest, and the indentation in my abdomen where medical tubes were inserted. I was teased about it and would come home crying. My mom told me to tell them that I'm unique and have two belly buttons. As weird as I thought that was it WORKED! From then on kids were fascinated by it and no longer teased me about it.

I am an empath. I didn't recognize it until recently and I'm finding ways to cultivate it. I'm a sensitive person by nature, but I typically don't allow others to see that. I thought I was just paying attention to the signals (expressions and body language) from others. There are many types of empaths: Emotional, Physical, Intellectual, Intuitive and Spiritual. I consider myself a combo of emotional / intuitive. I resonate with others through their feelings as if they were my own. Intuitively, I get a visual thought about the meaning.

My twin sister is sensitive, like myself. I believe she also is empathic. We seem to know things about people and are sensitive to their energy. Looking back at some memories, I can recall a time when we were younger, out playing with neighborhood kids down the street. There was a moment when I was looking away and my twin had a verbal disagreement with another kid, which led to my sister's face being deeply scratched. As soon as it happened, I looked up and into my sister's eyes, and we both began crying profusely and at the same time started running in the direction towards home. I felt her pain as it became mine and we cried together in unison. We would keep looking forward and then look back at each other while we were running and crying. Then suddenly we both looked at each other again began laughing hysterically. The pain went away and we both kept laughing together the rest of the way home.

My parents were of different faiths. My mother was Catholic and my father is an Eckist (Eckankar). Eckankar teaches spiritual exercises to connect with God through Divine Spirit (the ECK), which can be heard as sound and seen as light. Techniques for personal experience with dreams, past lives, soul travel and your spiritual destiny. Eckankar means "Co-worker with God" to develop your relationship with the Divine. By applying divine guidance to everyday life and your journey home to God, the full experience of God is possible in this lifetime! One thing I want to point out is that even though my mom was Catholic she, along with my sisters and I, sometimes have prolific dreams about people/events. So I guess these traits were inherited.

My father agreed to have us raised Catholic, at my mother's

insistence. He rarely discussed his beliefs with us out of respect for my mother. However, every now and again he would give snippets of info about his dreams, or when walking on the beach one day we saw those tiny colorful clams that appear when the wave recedes and then they would dig themselves back into the sand again before the next wave. He would say things like, "We all evolve like these little clams and every living thing has a soul." Profound and wacky thoughts to a Catholic kid who lived in a conservative community. As I grew older (teenage years and adulthood) I pushed away from religion. I questioned my faith and spirituality. I just didn't jive with it, so I left it behind. It took a few decades to come back around and while it's not the same format so to speak, I have a renewed sense of God and spirituality.

Our small Catholic school taught about God, religion and the fear of sin, but we were not taught empathy, kindness nor compassion towards others in our day-to-day existence. See, because I went to a small school it was very concentrated into groups. You either fit in or you didn't. Well you can guess when you are different you don't fit in. I was teased about my physical features and for who I was, first verbal, then physical. I could never understand why they were so thrilled when my twin or I were hurt. I developed a thick skin, when kids called me names or excluded me, I pretended to be OK. My pleas for help fell on deaf ears. I felt worthless and depressed, became disconnected, and retreated within myself due to the extreme bullying. I would also get easily annoyed with my twin. I didn't want to be around her, everything bothered me. She was a mirror to me. At the time I didn't recognize it, but all the stuff that annoyed me about her were the things I didn't like about myself.

I found comfort in creating art, painting and drawing. Lots of daydreaming took place. My love of nature was also cultivated, as I would go into the woods to explore and just let my senses be consumed with Mother Nature. It was very grounding and healing for me. I wanted to stop hiding who I was and began expressing myself.

School didn't allow for much self-expression, because we had uniforms and a dress code. I would try subtle things here and there. I would wear pink flats with a navy blue uniform. By the way, don't get dressed in the dark. A few times I wore two different colored shoes. I started getting expressive with my hair. However I don't recommend using an entire bottle of Sun-In. While having my hair dyed orange now is fun, back then it was more of a big oops! Especially since I was trying to bleach it blonde. Ask me to show you my sixth grade school photo sometime and you will get a good laugh!

We all have to come into our own at some point. Maybe it was hormones of teenage emotions or maybe I was sick and tired of the way I was treated from so many for so long and finally reached my breaking point at the end of my time in Catholic school and for the first time in my life I boldly stood up for myself. And it finally stopped. It all just stopped. Maybe success is measured in moments. How we can overcome life obstacles and continue to move forward.

In high school I finally was able to make artistic expressions through different mediums. I didn't flourish due to my doubts about my abilities and comparisons with others. Man! Self-doubt is kryptonite! My artwork was unusual. I couldn't quite master traditional techniques, so my work was a bit more abstract. I had an art teacher named Mr. Jacoby who really opened up my love and appreciation for art. He was convinced that I was an artist and thought I had skills and talent to attend art school and wanted me to build my portfolio and pursue it. I didn't believe in myself to move forward. During that time I had a TV production class, and when I picked up that video camera I was hooked! I was always running around school with a video camera and making short clips. My love for visual storytelling began.

"God's gift to you is more talent and ability than you will ever use in one lifetime. Your gift to God is to develop and utilize as much of that talent and ability as you can, in this lifetime."
~ Steve Bow

I graduated from The Pennsylvania State University with a degree in Communications/Film Production in the spring of '95 (the most expensive piece of paper I own!) A few weeks later I was on a cross-country drive with my then boyfriend (now hubby) to California, to work on films. I always loved movies and how the visual component could tell the story, and decided I wanted to become a Cinematographer one day. I worked my way up from intern, loader, 2nd AC to Focus Puller, and a teeny tiny bit of operating (when given the chance), on films, music videos, TV shows and a wide expanse of content. There weren't many women working in the camera department. I hustled to build relationships and worked as hard as I could. Made lots of mistakes and developed my technical skills, as I gained experience. My intuition was key in my ability to successfully pull focus. It became natural for me.

Many people believe that the movie industry is very liberal. I can tell you that it most certainly isn't. I either got work because I was a woman or I didn't get work because I was a woman. Men in the camera department said that women shouldn't do anything technical. It's ludicrous to think that it's such a Boys Club but WOW OH WOW it most certainly is. Ohhh the stories I could tell you! I was known for my strength and hard work ethic. On a show where I was the only woman in the department, I became known as someone who could do everything because I would not only handle my job, but the specific jobs of two others within the department without complaint and no support from production nor my male department heads. I worked harder than any man on that crew because I had to and everyone knew it. As a nod some fellow crew members once got me a book How To Do Everything (that gave me a good chuckle). One can only work like that for so long before becoming disenchanted. 12-15+ hour workdays and no personal life didn't help. I forgot my passion and just worked instead of working towards the creative. You know the adage "work to live instead of live to work."

After several years in the film industry, with overwork and my passion being burned out, I wanted to be involved in more personal creative endeavors. I started a wedding and event planning business on the side. I took courses, volunteered to gain knowledge and experience, and became active in the industry to educate and develop industry standards – all while still working 12-15 hours per day in the film industry. The weddings eventually took over as I became more in demand for my services. I basically jumped in with both feet. It wasn't something I planned for my life. I felt that I failed accomplishing my goal of being a cinematographer, but sometimes failure is a stepping stone towards the future.

I've planned hundreds of weddings over the years, experienced many different customs, cultures and religions, worked with some amazing clients and event professionals that I've developed close relationships with over the years. I've learned so much about people and how listening is so important to understanding others. One theme that stood out over the years, are the comments from my clients – who always said the same thing. That I always seemed to know exactly what they needed, and that I always made them feel calm. Looking back I can see that intuition played a huge role in that "knowing." Being a part of making others' dreams come true impacted my life in a very positive way. I am a top-notch wedding planner. I'm confident in saying that. But no matter how hard I worked, how perfect the wedding turned out, how much I sacrificed for my clients, I felt unaccomplished because my success didn't translate into the financial prosperity I wanted or expected. I seemed to just struggle getting paid what I'm worth.

And then a new chapter in my life started. On August 3, 2009 at 9:38 am I met the most perfect human. He had a full head of wild hair and a set of lungs to match. I smiled and cried as I met him. My kiddo was a big talker from a young age. I think he started speaking complete sentences when he came out of the womb! Always on the move and very perceptive. When my son reached elementary school he began to struggle emotionally. He would get easily frustrated and impulsive in his reactions to situations and people around him. It was never anything drastic, so the red flags didn't go up yet. In first grade he greatly struggled with behavior and emotions in the classroom. So much so that he became suspended. I couldn't believe that they actually suspend six year olds. I was beginning to feel stressed and like a failure as a parent. By second grade he was struggling so much in peer relationships as well as the classroom we had him assessed and he was diagnosed as ADHD. My heart sank. I was confused and concerned for my son. What did this mean for him socially, academically and his future? I didn't know what to do next. There are many obstacles and stigmas that kids with ADHD face. I am committed to finding ways to help him.

We tried Neurofeedback, behavioral therapy, and childhood psychology, which looking back I think he was just too young to benefit from. Chiropractic (NST), nutrition, probiotics, supplements, essential oils and medication are all part of the arsenal. Learning about essential oils and seeing benefits from daily use I was introduced to my future friend Bree Noall from Utah, who came to California once a month to do Foot Zone treatments. Someone described it like a foot massage and reflexology but way better. I was like YEAAAH! Sign me up! I love having my feet rubbed.

Foot Zone Therapy is a healing modality that accesses circulatory, lymphatic, nervous, skeletal, endocrine, digestive, respiratory, reproductive, muscular systems as well as emotional and spiritual self (bodies) through signal points on the feet to correct and renew the body at a cellular level. The foot zoner accesses the energy pathways through the body's meridians. The meridians end in your extremities - hands, ears, tongue and feet - and go up and down your body.

Every time Bree would come into town I would get a foot zone. I always felt great afterwards. At one point I asked my son if he wanted one and he agreed. OMG he just loved it! He was smiling, content and complete mush! Bree knew exactly what was going on with him by just working on his feet! I didn't tell her anything and she just knew. I was kind of astounded. She helped him to balance and the results were wonderful. Bree invited me to take a class she was offering to become a Foot Zoner. Of course I laughed it off. I loved having my feet worked on but hell no was I going to be interested in touching other people's feet. But then I stopped and thought for a moment and said, "Why not?!" The first thing my son Jackson did was get into a chair and put his feet up for me to work on. I laughed and told him it will take me a while to learn how to zone but I would practice on him regularly.

Coming back to spirituality has increased my senses and intuition. I am reconnecting with my true self and my connection with God. My empathic abilities are more intense physically as well as emotionally. Life transformation can be messy and painful. In order for growth, I need to acknowledge and work on what I can change and let go of what I can't. I became a Certified Foot Zone and Emotion Code Practitioner so that I can help my son and others live a happy and balanced life. My son has benefited so much. He is less anxious, is more calm and focused. He is able to better process and discuss his emotions, and I now have an additional tool to help him with sports injuries and health ailments if they arise. I never imagined that I would be able to have such an impact helping my son.

All the life struggles, obstacles, success and failures got me where I am today. My identity is not in these struggles but rather what I've learned along the way to overcome them. So maybe I haven't yet found my life purpose. But what if the pursuit of our life purpose IS our life purpose?

"Life is a journey, not a destination." ~ Ralph Waldo Emerson

I don't know where this journey will lead me as I continue on this crazy ride called life. I know there are going to be ups and downs, and some loops thrown in for good measure. But I think I'm securely buckled in and I'm going to raise my hands in the air and scream with laughter and enjoy the ride!

I think Maya Angelou said it best. "We delight in the beauty of the butterfly, but rarely admit the changes it has gone through to achieve that beauty." May all of you spread your wings and achieve the beauty of your complete self you are destined to be!

MARY'S LIFE HACKS

🎙 Wake up with positive intention and appreciation.

🎙 Positive thoughts create positive action. Thoughts are things. Surround yourself with people, places and things that are uplifting.

🎙 Continue to learn new things and grow from them.

🎙 Let Go and Let God.

🎙 Create JOY in your life. Jesus. Others. You.

🎙 End the day in prayer and gratitude.

🎙 Listen to your intuition. Hands down every time it's never wrong.

🎙 Don't sweat the small stuff.

Mary Sushinski is a Certified Practitioner in Foot Zone Therapy and Emotion Code. She is an essential oil wellness advocate. She has a Bachelors of Art degree in Film Production and Communications from The Pennsylvania State University. She earned her designation as a "Professional Bridal Consultant" from The Association of Bridal Consultants, and was Director of Education for ABC-GLA (Association of Bridal Consultants – Greater Los Angeles). Mary has published events, articles, inspirational photo shoots in wedding magazines such as *Brides, The Knot, Grace Ormonde* and *Bride World,* and does public speaking on all things wedding and wedding planning. A connoisseur of good food, wine and friends, she designs custom artisan jewelry for her clients that uplift the mind and the senses.

Connect with Mary
www.Sol-Balance.com • IG @SolBalanced
www.OccasionsEventProduction.com • IG @OccasionToRemember

Impact
THE WORLD
with your
unique
TALENTS!

~ Susie Augustin

Lessons from the Rooftop
by Joe Casas, MSW

"Why did you come up here?" my eleventh-grade student asked as she quietly sat on her house roof wearing her hijab. She was not aware that her mother had called me, concerned that her daughter did not want to attend school anymore.

Feeling a little anxious, I replied, "I wanted to see what you see." In disbelief to see me climbing her roof, she responded, "You're crazy!" I smiled and laughed for a second as I said, "I think you're right."

I mean, what high school guidance counselor climbs the back fence of a house to meet with their student on the roof? It's not in my job description, but in this case and on this day, the roof became the classroom, the scenery became the curriculum and "building a connection" became the common core. I sat perhaps about ten feet from her on the warm tiles as I began to become aware of the beautiful horizon. I couldn't help but gaze at the San Gabriel Mountains towards the north, the top of the Crystal Cathedral to the south, the tip of Disneyland's Matterhorn ride to the east and the beginning of a beautiful sunset to the west. It became a very surreal moment.

Not once did we speak about school, credits, attendance, graduation or the need to be in school. It was not the time and certainly not the place. This moment became about validating her feelings and respecting her emotional equity with an understanding that every behavior has a reason. It became another opportunity to exercise the values that are fundamental to any helping profession; Service, Social Justice, Importance of Human Relationships, Integrity, Competence, Dignity and Worth of the Person.

For a second, the Imposter Syndrome (thoughts and feelings of professional inadequacy) attempted to take over my mind. I questioned my competency and judgement. Dr. Angelica

Gutierrez, Business Professor at Loyola University refers to this insecurity, "...as a sign of stepping into greatness," and recommends taking ownership of the syndrome.

As we continued our conversation, I remember thinking at one point, "It's because she's on the rooftop that she will do great things." Years later, I realized her isolation and escape to her roof was a form of practicing mindfulness. Seeing the world through her eyes gave me the opportunity to connect and understand.

"I come up here to get away from everyone," she said with a disgusted and disappointed tone.

"I don't blame you, everyone needs a rooftop," I responded with reassurance and in agreement.

While many said to her, "you're crazy", for escaping or hiding on the roof, it was a place where she became healthier and wiser. She had found a scenic and beautiful place where silence and her thoughts peacefully met. It was her "emotional home." Do you have an emotional home you can go to?

After that meeting, I didn't see her back at school. Actually, I didn't hear back from them for over a year. I felt a sense of failure for not saying the right things at the moment, but my focus was getting to her heart. It's been said, "To get to the heart of the problem, you must get to the problem of the heart." Dr. Rios, professor of Sociology at University of Santa Barbara once said, "When you teach to the heart, the mind will follow."

Nevertheless, I remembered she had spoken about her decision to one day prove everyone wrong. She spoke defeated, yet at times she allowed me to see her spirit emerging from the ashes like a Phoenix. Her qualities outweighed her deficiencies, as it is true with many students once we see beyond their behavior. I asked myself, how can someone want something so badly and not do it? I was reminded of how the decision process works.

Three Frogs

There are three frogs sitting on a lily pad on a beautiful pond. Two of them **decided** to jump in the water, how many are left sitting on the lily pad? It's not algebra or a trick question. It's simple, three frogs sitting on a lily pad, two decide to jump. How many are left?

While most people would say that the answer is one frog, there's a more profound response. It has to do with our decision-making process. It seems that we have been conditioned to believe that a decision is completed once our thought process has conceived the desired goal. In other words, if I say I have decided to lose ten pounds, but don't work towards it, it was simply a "decision thought."

Things don't happen just because you decided, *goals* happen because there was action after the decision was made. Many of us, I would assume, know someone or have heard someone say, "I want to quit smoking, I want to quit drinking, I want to graduate, I want to travel this year, I want to lose weight," and so on. Although they are noble goals and desires, the decision is not completed, it's just a thought. To make it happen, a decision must be followed through with action, always.

So, let's go back to the pond. The question then becomes, did those two frogs jump? Since they only decided, it doesn't mean that they jumped. The answer is actually, three. Three frogs are still left. They decided to jump but never did. What decisions have you made that you haven't acted upon? What dreams are still on hold, that all it takes is your actions to make it happen? I recently read a quote by Dr. Ryan Lowery, "Don't fear failure, fear being in the exact same place next year as you are today."

Rising from the Ashes

Over a year went by and at this point and I had transferred high schools to work the ILC (Independent Learning Center), a dropout prevention program on the east side of town in Anaheim, CA. One morning, out of the corner of my eye, I noticed someone entering the classroom. As she walked closer to me, wearing her hijab and a determined smile she said, "I looked for you and they told me you were here now, I want to graduate, can I enroll with you?"

With joy and overwhelming satisfaction to see her I replied, "Of course, welcome to my rooftop."

She smiled from ear to ear and said, "I thought about what you said that day." I knew what "that day" meant. She had returned to someone who valued and believed in herself. I am reminded that as human beings, we all have two basic innate needs; to love and to be loved. Schools can never forget about the human spirit, its strength and its resiliency.

It has been said, "You can lead a horse to the water, but you can't make him drink it." Consequently, we tend to stop at that point. The next step can be a life-changing step, and that is to make them thirsty. I realized I had not led her to the water, but instead, somehow, I had made her thirsty. When thirsty, eventually they will come to the water on their own. Dr. Pedro Noguera, professor at UCLA and Director, Center for the Transformation of Schools states, "Great teachers know how to teach people, not just the curriculum." We are all teachers in some way, but we should never stop being students first.

I've often heard that our youth are the leaders of tomorrow. I refuse to believe that. I've seen them leading today in so many ways. I saw one leading from the rooftop. Adults, including educators, often ask, "What is wrong with the youth of today?" but the more compassionate, healthier and optimistic question is, "What is right with the youth of today?" When approaching children and adolescents from an asset based model vs. a deficit perspective, I have learned that it validates their strengths and reinforces their value regardless of their performance, behavior, and aptitude.

I will never forget these and other lessons that soon, (2020), I will continue to expand in my book, *Lessons from the Rooftop – from Impossible to I'm Possible.*

JOE'S SUCCESS TIPS

 Deny the Less for the Greater: Give your time and attention to what has the greater long-term value.

Everywhere you go should be a better place because you're there: You are important and valuable.

Learn to see the world through other people's eyes: You will often gain from an additional perspective.

Your treasure is where your heart is. Give your time and energy to what's important.

It's not about how you start, but how you finish. Get help then become the help to someone one day.

Find your "rooftop." Self-time doing mindfulness or prayer will boost your inner-peace and balance.

FAITH: The constant and stubborn promise that with God's abundant help, we will overcome.

Joe Casas is an effective, motivational, and multi-talented High School Guidance Counselor. He earned a Masters Degree (USC 95') in Social Work with an emphasis in mental health and a PPS Credential. He is a dynamic speaker and has presented in numerous student, parent, education, and church conferences. In 2018, his personal artwork was exhibited at the Inaugural Congressional Hispanic Heritage Month celebration. He is currently casted for the role of "Lucas" in the theater production, StanD, and has performed singing at the iconic Steven's Steakhouse in Los Angeles. Joe is passionate about our youth, life, and his faith.

Connect with Joe
FB Joe Casas • IG @JoeMCasas

Transformation For A Fit Body, Mind And Soul

by Maria Mizzi

Visualizing my future self and owning a positive attitude led to life changing transformations and eventually, a new rewarding career. One day while sitting in my office, feeling unhealthy and unhappy, I took a rare moment to wonder. I was finishing up the day at the office and was ready to go home. The Oscars were about to start and I couldn't wait to watch. The Oscars are always around my birthday, so I started to think about the past year and what was happening in my life. I then found myself imagining I was at the Oscars walking down the Red Carpet feeling graceful, glamorous, gleeful, genuine and glowing. I wanted to feel all of that. I wondered, "How can I feel that way every time I walk into a room?" God, how I really wanted to show up for life full of energy and confidence every day. But I did not feel this way at all. I felt tired, trapped and troubled.

Not long before, I had been working in finance in New York. I worked long days, had a long commute and zero time to *really* take care of myself. Because the job was so intense, I became a "grabber." I grabbed a muffin (from my weekend shopping at Costco) on my way out the door in the morning. I later learned these oversized muffins were full of empty calories, mostly from carbohydrates, sugar and unhealthy fats. Basically, I was eating a cupcake without the frosting for breakfast every morning. No wonder I was dragging my butt into the office daily, I was already crashing from the sugar overload. I usually grabbed lunch at a fast food joint near the office and my go-to was McDonalds or Taco Bell. Some days I'd grab a couple slices of pizza. I think you can guess how I felt after those choices. I always seemed to feel like I needed a nap after lunch, my brain was foggy too, so I grabbed a pick-me-up snack out of the vending machine in the afternoon. By the time I got home I was so exhausted that I grabbed a bowl of cereal, a piece of pizza or something easy like that and went to bed where I grabbed a few hours of sleep.

With the high stress, long hours, sitting all day and eating poorly, I gained 40 pounds in one year. I developed anxiety from my poor body image and the food I was eating. I had heartburn every day. And, of course, I didn't fit into any of my clothes. At that point I was exhausted, felt sick and felt like I looked...bad. Basically, my energy left and took my confidence with it.

I couldn't take it any longer. None of these burdens were necessary, it just made my life toxic in numerous other ways. I was ready to gain back my power and lose the weight I was carrying around both physically and emotionally. So, I spent the next year trying to feel better. I tried the latest diets. Did you know there are over 200 types of diets out there? I may have tried them all. I got gym memberships but didn't feel comfortable in my own skin or have enough energy to actually show up consistently. Then, I saw doctors. I spent countless hours with numerous different specialists only to be recommended pills that made me sick...you name it, I tried it, but nothing worked. I was totally frustrated that I couldn't lose the weight, but I was even more upset that I just didn't feel good or look the way I wanted to. I kind of lost my spunk.

One day I decided enough was enough. I knew in my heart there was a better way and I was determined to figure it out. Driving home one night (after another long day at the office) I was sitting in traffic and started to examine my life. Then, I heard a voice from within myself. She said, "It's your time to come back, to feel good, have fun and be you. Remember when you were the happiest person you knew?" Strangely enough, I answered back. For some reason, I grabbed the fat that had developed around my middle and said, "It's time to get rid of this, I don't need it. It's weighing me down literally and figuratively. I must get back to feeling good; I need to get ahold of my health and raise my happiness. It's time to end this struggle and find harmony with myself. To live a life of ease, joy and grace." I felt renewed in that present moment. I deserved to be healthy and feel good. I was ready to take a big leap.

That night I got home and enrolled in my first wellness class.

I became a seeker of knowledge about nutrition, psychology and spirituality. Just a few months into my studies, I realized I could heal myself. I learned enough to lose the weight and gain back my resilience, energy and confidence. I lost the 40 pounds, had energy like a kid playing in the park and had the resilience to keep going. I started to live a vibrant, heathy and joyous lifestyle!

But I didn't stop there. I continued my education and began teaching what I had learned to others. I changed my career path in the process. This change was not something that I consciously thought of, but what happened as a result of my quest for health and well-being. I opened my transformational nutrition practice, moved to California and continued to learn how to help people transform themselves without deprivation. I finally felt light, energized, confident and abundant.

What I discovered in all my work, research and through hundreds of clients' transformations, is that it's a lifestyle of confidence and energy that we want, because the bottom line is, we really want to have that "Red Carpet entrance" all day, every day. And it's not just about calories in, calories out and the number on a scale; it's how you feel in your mind, body and soul consistently. That's what it's all about. So, I created what I call 'The Confidence and Energy Cycle', comprised of simple shifts that create dramatic results. A trifecta that includes nutrition, exercise and selfcare.

What I discovered in the area of nutrition, is that when you become aware and conscious of what you are eating, you begin to feel better. When you are eating for energy, you naturally feel more energetic. I ate foods that fueled my body with nutrients. And guess what, the pounds disappeared! I lost the weight but still wasn't ready to make my Red Carpet entrance. There was more work to do.

Another simple shift I made was to move my body with exercise that felt good and made me stronger. I started to take five-minute walking breaks at work and got up a little earlier in the morning to exercise to a short strength training workout video from home. It was nothing drastic, but it was a conscious step to move a little more, get my heart pumping and my body stronger every day. I made it super easy, doing it for only 5-20 minutes, a few times a day. I did this without fail every day. It was several minutes of focused movement to improve my body inside and out consistently. I have a secret, here's why it worked...exercise is cumulative. It all adds up. A few times a day moving at my office for five minutes and a 20-minute workout at home meant that I was moving with purpose for 45 minutes a day.

And guess what happens when you move just a little bit more with purpose, you start to feel better! I started to feel good and could see and feel myself transforming. My confidence seemed to improve and every week I felt stronger. My muscles started to notice the movement and my body started to change. The body-mind connection began, my head noticed too. I was no doubt thinking more clearly. I no longer had those afternoon slumps. And a few months later, I had more physical and mental energy, real vibrant "I'm alive" energy inside and out, and I felt good!

And the best part? I felt GREAT about feeling good and about taking care of myself! I started to stand a little taller and hold my head a bit higher. I also seemed to bounce back from difficult situations in the office quickly; I was regaining my mental strength, too. I was blown away by the simplicity of my new daily habits and the amazing results they created.

I learned that eating well and exercising made perfect sense. Doing more of each is logical for any transformation. But I also knew that diet and exercise were only 2/3 of the picture. There was another piece to this puzzle to sustain this transformation long term. I researched and studied the link between nutrition, physiology and psychology. Simply stated, you have to take care of your head so that the other shifts make sense and can be sustained. Change of diet and exercise won't help long term if you don't change your thoughts. It's just as important to feed your mind with positive fueling thoughts as it is to feed your body with fueling foods.

That's when I created 'The Confidence and Energy Cycle'. I was not only making a healthy change, but keeping it and making it a lifestyle. I followed the cycle of nutrition, exercise and self-care. When you eat better you begin to feel good. As you start to feel good you want to move more. Then, as you eat nourishing foods and move your body more, you have more energy and confidence. So, you continue to eat well and move.

I began to reinforce the feeling of my food and exercise success with the knowledge I learned about positive psychology. I started to build back up my resilience by visualizing my future self and owning a positive attitude. I was feeding my mind with positive self-talk and what I thought about myself. I started to journal about my day, my food and my thoughts.

Did you know we have about 60,000 thoughts a day, 95% are the same and about 80% are negative? Usually, we are saying those negative things about our self. The good news is that I studied the best ways to turn down the negative self-talk and turn up the positive self-talk. It's easier to turn around than you think. With journaling and noticing my thoughts, I was able to kick the destructive habit of negative self-talk to the curb and maintain a long-term confident attitude. I started to answer those negative thoughts back and distanced myself from them. I stopped playing those same destructive thoughts over and over and added more positive activities into my life, like being in nature, talking with people who I enjoyed and doing more of the things I loved.

On my own journey to rise up to my new standards of health and happiness, I discovered a method that worked for me. I found that it was about creating a personalized nutrition and fitness plan that moved beyond just the basics of food and exercise. I took time to find out what was truly going on in my life; what was causing the heaviness, dis-ease and unhappiness I was experiencing. Alas, I found true transformation for my whole self: body, mind and soul, to create long-lasting results. Taking care of your body, mind and inner guidance system are what is needed to live life full out and truly enjoy a life of peace and positivity.

That's a major part of what I teach and coach now. We can eat the right stuff but if we don't give our mind and soul good stuff, the body will suffer along with it. You can address it all, that's why I created transformational nutrition...it's the whole self that needs to participate (mind, body and soul). Stay well, be happy and live full out! That's the winning formula!

When you set a strong, committed intention to live a healthy, authentic life – you will create the right people, opportunities and results in your life that will support your well-being and personal success.

MARIA'S TIPS TO SUCCESS

🎤 Eat well. Food is energy. Fuel your body with nourishing foods and water.

🎤 Exercise. Movement empowers you. Consistency is key.

🎤 Love yourself. Create positive affirmations, see yourself with eyes of love. Look in the mirror and say, "I love you".

🎤 Gratitude is an attitude! Be thankful for all you have now.

🎤 Observe your own thoughts. Think about what you're thinking about.

🎤 Surround yourself with people and community that help you grow.

🎤 Decide to feel good. Happiness is a choice you make!

Maria Mizzi is a Certified Transformational Nutrition Coach, Speaker, weight loss specialist and fitness expert. Maria is the co-author of the #1 bestseller *Passionistas*, the creator of The Beach Physique Method and the True Transformation Program that has helped people create simple shifts in their health and life. Maria has coached and inspired thousands of women and men, creating permanent changes in their lives through transformational nutrition and healthy lifestyle habits. She has over 20 years of experience coaching and training clients from TV personalities to entrepreneurs and busy executives helping them transform their body, mind and life.

Connect with Maria
www.MariaMizzi.com • FB & IG @MariaMizziCoach

TRIUMPH OVER TRAGEDY

by Barbi Jolliffe

We were a busy, normal and happy traditional Catholic family. My five kids were into dance, music and martial arts. I worked part-time and always made sure they had a home-cooked meal. We thought we were doing everything right. However, even families that seem to have it all can experience tragedy and shock.

Our two sons were abused by our Catholic priest in rural Northern California. My oldest son came forward after the priest died. By this time, the priest had him addicted to drugs and alcohol. My youngest son started having seizures, my daughters were falling apart, and my husband was working hours away, only coming home on the weekends.

I struggled with this for over a year until I pushed to move to the Bay Area where my husband was working. I knew I had to save my family. The resources I had in our small remote area were limited for the help I knew we needed. My youngest son kept ending up in the hospital due to the many seizures he had, while my oldest son had gone to a recovery center in the Bay Area. My oldest daughter lived in Napa, and my middle daughter was in college and moving with us. We were there for two weeks when my youngest son had a seizure that caused him to hit his head as he fell. As a result, his leg became numb for nine months. He was on crutches, put on home study and had seizures almost daily. We were in an area where there were lots of options and alternatives, so we started looking into all of them.

And wouldn't you know, miracles can happen. Slowly his leg started waking up. One day, his dad put him in his wetsuit and took him to swim in the ocean. His leg suddenly felt better and he walked off of the sand carrying his crutch. It was definitely a miraculous time for us.

Later, my husband took a job in Southern California. My son

started to pour himself into music, and we hoped it would help with the seizures. My son suddenly came forward at this time and told us that he too had been abused by our family priest. His seizures continued to get worse after we moved, with him often falling to the ground and hitting his head almost daily. His new therapist was able to help him thrive, but the doctors still couldn't find the cause of the seizures. In the middle of dealing with this, we were also in a lawsuit against the Catholic Church. Life was overwhelming!

However, intuitively I knew we were beginning to start healing. I began looking into everything I could to help heal me and my family. I started going to seminars and making great friendships. These groups and the women I have met have been my saving grace in getting me to where I am today. I couldn't get enough teachings about self-love, staying strong, letting go and finding your true calling. I would bring home everything I was learning and teach it to my family. They were very receptive and learned along with me. I saw my kids becoming stronger; things were slowly turning around. It was then that I realized what my true passion in life was.

I took a course on confidence that changed my life and also joined a mastermind group. It was so wonderful to have the support and friendship of these women as we all moved through changes in our lives. I became a certified life coach with a focus on sexual abuse and trauma recovery. My purpose is helping abuse survivors and their loved ones through this awful time in life, and helping them to find joy and happiness again.

When my oldest son first came forward I found SNAP (Survivors Network of those Abused by Priests) online. We still lived in rural Northern California. They gave me so much support over the phone. When we moved to the Bay Area, I was able to start attending meetings and really started to heal while telling our story and listening to others. After moving to Southern California and my younger son came forward, SNAP was fantastic as always and helped me through the worst of it. I became a leader with SNAP and now co-lead a monthly meeting and lead a virtual meeting for families. I take phone calls and emails from survivors and family members. I also lead breakout sessions at our annual conferences and speak on behalf of SNAP at events. SNAP is the oldest and largest sexual abuse support group. They have been an invaluable resource for me and thousands of others through this journey. I am now a leader in this 31-year-old worldwide organization and we help all victims of sexual abuse. I am very dedicated to helping survivors and their loved ones heal.

Now, my oldest daughter and her family live in Northern California. My middle daughter is an ER nurse and engaged. My oldest son is still struggling. He has been in and out of several recovery centers and sober living homes. He still chooses to abuse drugs and does his own thing. He knows that when he is ready to get clean and choose a different way of life, we are here. This is my biggest daily heartache. My youngest daughter just graduated from college and is pursuing her dream career. My youngest son is a fantastic musician and songwriter. He struggles but continues to work on himself in therapy. I am thankful for these fantastic kids. It has been a long journey to this point.

One of the other traumas of this abuse happening to my family is the loss of my 30 year marriage. My husband and I worked together on what the kids needed, but the guilt you feel as a parent freezes you and we stopped being a team. Starting over has been extremely hard but good for both of us.

Recently, I had another huge challenge. I fell and broke my right arm. The healing has been hard and I still have a long road ahead of me. During my recovery I wrote an online coaching course. I know in my heart that everything will be OK. I have been through so much and keep coming out stronger. I am following my passion, my body is healing and I know I will find love again.

BARBI'S SELF-CARE TIPS

 Make a list every day of three things that brought you joy.

Visualize yourself where you want to be.

Start a journal. Write down your overwhelming thoughts and feelings. Allow yourself to express everything. Take time to read it back. Now ask yourself, "Do I need to hang on to these thoughts and feelings anymore? How would changing these make a difference in my life?" From there, write down happy thoughts and positive things you want in your life.

Say NO to others and YES to yourself.

Forgive yourself, love yourself, take care of yourself and find joy in the little things.

Barbi Jolliffe is the mother of five (two abused sons) and grandmother of three. While healing with her family, she discovered her passion for helping other survivors and their loved ones. She became a Certified Life Coach, author and speaker who specializes in helping men, women, teens and children recover from trauma, overcome hardships and triumph over tragedies. Barbi is an expert at helping parents of abuse victims heal and move past the guilt and trauma. This includes abuse, rape, PTSD, anxiety, family issues, parenting and more.

Connect with Barbi
www.BarbiJolliffeCoaching.com • FB Triumph Over Tragedy

EACH OF US
HAS A
CALLING
that we can find the more
conscious
we become.

~ Kim Somers Egelsee

INNER STRENGTH
by Tara Vevante

The world around me literally stopped. I received a phone call that my 11-year-old son was in a terrible car accident caused by a drunk driver. I felt my heart rip out of my chest. This minute was the longest of my life until I heard my son say he was okay but wanted his mom. I could finally breathe again. I rushed to the hospital to be with him and there he was, joking around and smiling. His only complaint was a stomachache and a slight headache. I was so relieved it was nothing serious that could be seen.

At a young age, I lost my mother; she was hit by a drunk driver. The memories that were brought up increased my stress level and little did I know, triggered my PTSD. As a mom, I felt like I had to put my feelings aside and focus on my son.

About a week later my son complained of a headache and the lights being too bright. After an examination, my son was diagnosed with a concussion. He had to see a concussion specialist every other week for the next 8 months. At one point, my son was rushed to the hospital in an ambulance due to a possible seizure, as he could not be woken up. That felt like the longest car ride of my life. My mind raced with only negative thoughts, that my baby was going to die or be in a coma. As a mother, all you want to do is protect your child, but there was nothing I could do; I felt so distraught. At the hospital, he had wires attached to his head and they were running tests on him. I was so amazed at how well he handled everything; he was so strong.

As for myself, I was strong on the outside for my son, but on the inside, I felt like my heart, brain and soul were in a blender. Through eye therapy it was discovered he had convergence insufficiency. We started home schooling along with 2-3 doctor appointments a week. I switched from day to night shifts to pay the bills.

As happy as I was to be at home and take care of my son, I realized I had slipped into a depression. I was tired, sad and just didn't have the gusto to live life. I realized my health was important too. I knew I had to pick myself back up.

At this time, I started taking a life coaching course and every morning for the next two months I would wake up, look at myself in the mirror and say, "If you were going to die today what would you regret the most?" Slowly, as I studied the course and asked myself this question, I was able to pull myself out of the depression and started to rebuild my life.

Auditing my life truly helped me as well. I wrote down what was filling up my time, and wrote what I *wanted* to fill up my time. Also, I decided the path I was in at my job at the time was not what I wanted. I recognized where my future would be if I stayed at that job so I left for a better opportunity, enabling me to focus on a new a future career as a life coach. This truly amazing thing happens when you feel like you have nothing to lose – you actually lose your fear for certain things! This is one of the greatest lessons I've learned in life.

I am a true believer in doing the right thing. Always do what is right, not what is easy. Sometimes you need to challenge yourself with a hard situation to really learn a lesson. And don't forget to cheer yourself on. Remember to be your biggest cheerleader and cheer yourself on for small things, too. Live your truth and speak your truth. Most of us live a life full of what others expect of us. Don't forget about who you are, and live your most truthful self.

TARA'S TIPS FOR SUCCESS

- Make lasting memories – Memories are something that cannot be taken away. I always enjoy talking about the fun memories I have made with the people I cherish and hold close to me.

- Drink water, eat veggies and get some fresh air – Your body is with you for the rest of your life; make sure you take care of yourself.

- Smile – Smiling is not only good for your immune system, but it's also infectious.

- Remember to eat the cake – Don't forget to enjoy life, we often take life so seriously that we forget to eat the cake.

Tara Vevante is a certified Ten Plus Life Coach and Certified Confidence Coach. She is truly grateful for her son, stepchildren, family and friends. She is passionate in helping others to find new ways to overcome their past or current emotional traumas and to uncover their most authentic selves. She is currently working on building her life coaching career and paving her own path in the world. Tara is always studying something new in her downtime as she believes you should never stop learning. "Always find the gifts in each day, life is too short to not spoil yourself."

Connect with Tara
FB Tara Vevante • IG @Get_Out_Of_The_Grind

COURAGE

Nelson Mandela said, "I learned that courage was not the absence of fear, but the triumph over it." Sometimes it is in our darkest, weakest, hardest moments, hardships and experiences that we have the opportunities to develop the bravest, boldest and strongest courage. It can be those make us or break us times that we choose courage over giving up, because we know we have it in us, and are meant to be inspiring examples and teachers for others.

Defining moments transform our lives and we have choices in which direction we go. Do we takes steps of courage to make change, despite the pain and circumstances, or do we stay stagnant, finding ways to numb ourselves to tolerate a situation? Being brave enough to change and evolve develops character, growth and strength. Strength can be physical, mental and spiritual. Life challenges increase inner strength and growth. The way you handle these experiences can take you further in life.

Courage can be experienced in day to day life with the chance to speak in public, save a life, write a book, handle a huge health issue, comfort a sick or hurt pet or family member, with loss, or with tragedy. It is having strength in the face of fear or pain, facing extreme dangers or difficulties with audacity and valor. It is being able to evaluate your personal life and go through the process of being uncomfortable to get to the other side. It is making the conscious decision to make changes, and finding strength to help and empower others. This is true courage.

LIVE FOR EVERY MOMENT AND EXPERIENCE SUCCESS

by Elena Planas-Sena

Success, a term described for achievement, can be elusive and feel impossible to reach, yet it is attainable. Success is a relative term because the meaning is so different for everyone. Success can be described as a mind-set or attitude, which are behaviors that help lead to a completion of goals. However, most of us struggle to reach our versions of success due to the inability to learn life's lessons. How do you reach success when life throws obstacles and complications in your way?

In dealing with this question, I have created my personal definition of success by interweaving two main abstractions: failure and success. These abstractions go hand in hand. Without failure, how can you learn and appreciate the satisfaction of success? Failure and success have been pivotal instructors in my life.

Personally, success has always been something I have strived to reach, but life has proven to be demanding and managed to toss me the proverbial curveball, instead of an easy straight line. Life often says, "You don't always get what you want Elena; struggles are always present!"

Every difficulty and challenge has helped me press forward in life. My openness to failure has given me valuable insights into life lessons and opportunities. This is something that I learned early on in life and continue to experience every day. I know that without a doubt, my success has been positively influenced by my failures and letdowns. Because of those experiences, I CAN conquer everything that comes my way!

The Early Years

As an only child, I was blessed to grow up with two loving parents who were daily inspirations, positive influences and life instructors. They provided me with support, strength and laid the foundation for success in my life. My parents are the embodiment of all my professional goals and life goals. They showed me that hard work was the predictor of success coupled with laughter and lots of travel! They showed me how to work hard and keep persevering despite the trials and tribulations that fell in my path, and for that I am forever grateful.

At the age of 13, I encountered my first hurdle when I received the diagnosis of type 1 Diabetes: an autoimmune disease that affected my life in more positive ways than not. This was a challenging moment in my life that included constant sugar checks, insulin shots and a lifetime struggle that I would endure as a consequence of my body attacking itself.

At this time, I met a wonderful MD who taught me that overcoming my type 1 diabetes struggles would be "no big deal!" That small phrase changed my life forever. From that day forth, my "it's no big deal" attitude gave me the power to move forward despite the struggle. I believe that moving forward and onward while embracing your past struggles is one of the main predictors of success along with a little bit of cafécito.

Cafécito Time
Cafécito Time! A phrase, a statement, a moment in time, an occasion that has always permeated deep within me since I was a young girl. It is a moment shared by family, loved ones, lovers and friends...a wonderful time of self-reflection, a time to share thoughts, feelings, emotions, life goals and experiences.

When I was a little girl, Abuelita (my grandmother) introduced me to this life changing concoction of an aromatic coffee mixed with hot milk, a little bit of sweetness and lots of love. Since my introduction to this newfound wonder, my life has never been the same. For me, those moments tasting and savoring such a wonderful elixir meant that I was given the time to experience and learn from a person whom I admired.

Abuelita was a person who was not immune to the struggles of life. She battled through personal loss, life during a civil war, death of a few of her children and losing her husband to a terrible bus accident. Despite her struggles, she maintained a positive and hopeful disposition. Abuelita's positive outlook was something that I truly admired and that I work daily to attain. After drinking a cafécito, I can conquer the world and am reminded of a powerful woman who was able to overcome anything that life would throw at her.

Early Success
With my cafécito in hand and my "it's no big deal" attitude despite life's challenges, I was led to many moments of early success. I graduated from one of the top all girls' private high schools where I learned to become "a woman of great heart and right conscience." I then received Cum Laude honors at my university while achieving a bachelor's and master's degree in Speech Pathology in five years.

At the age of 23, I was an accomplished graduate and part of the 9% of people to hold a master's degree. Life was good. Shortly after graduating, I got hired to work at one of the top rehabilitation hospitals, giving me the opportunity to work on my craft. I began helping people regain their ability to communicate following a stroke, traumatic brain injury and spinal cord injury.

Fourteen years later, I'm still in love with my passion to help others. I still work hard every day to provide others with their voice, their ability to direct their life and reach their true potential following their own hardships and struggles. Working every day with my patients has taught me that to get what you want in life, you cannot stop or lose hope when hurdles are placed in your path. Opportunities are often found when disguised as a trial or test. It is a matter of searching and being open to reading the signals and finding the opportunities.

Family Support
Success, for me, has never been attained in isolation. My family, including my aunt, uncles and cousin/brother, have been by my side every step of the way. They have pointed me in

the right direction and have always believed in me, providing me with constant support. I consider myself to be a fortunate person who is always surrounded by love and guidance.

My husband positively impacted my life. He is a powerful role model, a fantastic father to my two wonderful stepchildren and a fabulous speech therapist. He is truly a person that shows me how vulnerability, laughter, appreciation, affection, humorous wit and an everlasting love can be wrapped up in one person. I realize that life puts people in your path that teach you lessons to help you reach greatness and overcome struggles.

Patience and strength are qualities that my husband exudes daily and are qualities that I learn from him each day. I feel lucky that I was able to find a life partner that not only complements me, but also challenges me to reach and surpass my standards.

I am also happy that I get to share in the experience of being a parent to two wonderful teenagers. My stepchildren are determined young individuals; they have great hearts and I learn from them daily. They are vocal, opinionated, driven, athletic and despite their challenges, live each day to its full potential. Every day I learn that being a parent is a life changing experience and it has been wonderful seeing how these two young individuals seize their moment, embrace life's challenges and rise to any occasion to reach their goals. I admire their strength and their drive to be wonderful people.

A New Challenge
Being a stepmother ignited my drive to have a child with my husband. Here is where we both encountered the most complicated hurdle in our path. I was given an unbelievable piece of information: Elena, you only have a five percent chance of being a mother.

I felt challenged and saddened, common emotions and feelings felt when given the diagnosis of infertility. My husband and I have continued to fight this struggle for the past three years, and it's a battle that no one really speaks about. Women suffering from infertility are silent warriors. Instead of curling up in a ball and crying, they exude confidence and strength. Struggling with infertility has taught me to be a resilient individual, a person who doesn't give up right away. Always in my mind are thoughts like, "This is no big deal" or "This too shall pass." I am always wondering if there will ever be a chance that I will carry a child of my own in addition to having the wonderful fulfillment of loving two wonderful stepchildren.

My husband and I decided to venture into the world of IVF (in vitro fertilization). A world that again not many people talk about. No one really talks about things that are "broken." No one (unless you are one that is also traversing this path) really talks about the never-ending struggle of being reproductively challenged. Millions of shots (okay, maybe not millions but it sure feels like it), people staring, questions being asked, looks headed in your direction when you've been married for longer than a year and are not pregnant, internal world wars in your own head telling you that you are not a "real woman" are just some of the things women like myself endure.

And Then Success
And then it happens. Success, or what seems to be success. A positive test revealing that with a little bit of science, possibilities do become endless. The negative thoughts escape; they become fleeting as life becomes consumed with positivity and ultimate happiness because of the possibility of the creation of this new life inside of you. Or so I thought.

Followed By Disaster
Fast forward six and half months. Complications arise. Blood pressures rise. Placental malfunctions occur. Hospitalization ensues with the possibility of death at my door. What seemed to be such a positive adventure quickly turned into a life-threatening ordeal. I remained positive throughout this tumultuous time and kept telling myself that everything was going to be okay; all the while not really knowing where my life was going. I never realized that life could take a nosedive and abruptly change.

The epitome of change happened right before my very eyes; an unfolding of emotions, turmoil overload, life leaving you in every sense of the phrase. A few simple words changed my destiny, "There is no heartbeat." My own heart fell hearing those words. My whole world, as I knew it, up until that point had gone as planned. All my dreams and plans of pregnancy, delivery and holding a representation of love that was going to be a beautiful combination of my husband and me, was a thought that had officially left the universe.

Life as I knew it had officially changed. From that moment on, I realized that I had to make alterations to my expectations. Mothers come in all forms. I am a stepmother and a mother to my angel who was too soon taken! My husband and I remain positive and realize that many roads are still available to us and we embrace every option that comes in our direction, i.e. use of a gestational carrier, adoption, etc. We believe that life opens doors, this too is no big deal and we will be parents yet again!

And Then The Transformation
Despite all the challenges, this chapter of my life is still moving forward. My life has ultimately been a transforming road with every experience including every trial, tribulation and happy moment intertwining. I have learned that to get what you want in life, you cannot stop or lose hope when things do not go your way.

Your beliefs are magnetic; they guide you to your ultimate destination. You make the final choice of your destiny. Purpose, drive, determination and motivation can help you along the path and journey to success.

The main ingredients to my success always remain the same: the knowledge that a choice always exists, my personal choice to maintain an "it's no big deal" attitude and a moment and time for cafécito, a drink that always brings me home.

ELENA'S SUCCESS TIPS

Remember everything that happens in life is really "no big deal." Always keep moving forward.

Always enjoy your time savoring a cafécito; spend your moments appreciating you!

Always enjoy your family; cherish your support system. Success is never attained in isolation.

Always remember that opportunities are often found when disguised as a trial or test. It is a matter of searching and being open to reading the signals and finding the opportunities.

Remember to embrace and accept every failure along with every success.

Success is not the absence of fear, it is the conquest of it.

Your beliefs are magnetic; they guide you to your ultimate destination. YOU make the final choice of your destiny.

Remember that success is a mindset. Believe in the power of you!

 **Elena M. Planas-Sena** was born in San Salvador, El Salvador and moved to Eagle Rock, CA at the age of three. She has bachelor's and master's degrees in Communication Disorders with a specialty in Speech Pathology from California State University, Los Angeles. Elena landed a job at the world-renowned Rancho Los Amigos National Rehabilitation Center as a Speech Language Pathologist. She has been at Rancho for the past 14 years and has worked on all services treating patients with devastating injuries. She also dedicates her time at local libraries providing speech and language workshops to families of school aged children.

Connect with Elena
IG @Elena_Love_Will

VIRAGO

by Kandice Astamendi

Virago. A woman who demonstrates a heroic, strong spirit, a female warrior. Each year I choose a word that really defines that year; last year was "intentional," and this year was "Virago."

I believe we all have a fierce warrior spirit inside each of us. How do we utilize or find it? It is actually much easier than you think. You already do it automatically, like when you protect your loved ones with a tenacity that no one questions. Without a doubt, you can be the biggest girly-girl and have a warrior spirit. What is that spirit? It's controlled, strong, confident and ready for anything that comes your way. For myself, it's important to stay positive, strong and to maintain a higher level of energy. Don't think for a minute I'm a bubbly ray of sunshine 24/7, but I *do* see the positive versus the negative as much as possible. Try to limit the negative and the vampires who suck your energy and positive vibes. Don't be afraid to distance yourself from them and seek out more positive people.

I'm not a writer by nature, can you tell? If you ask me to tell you a story or talk to a group, I'm all in. A lot of friends have asked how I've stayed positive and sane at one of my life's most painful moments. I lost my soulmate of over twenty-six years to one of the most devastating cancers on the planet. He had glioblastoma, an incurable brain cancer that the average lifespan is 14-16 months, with few that go past 5 years.

I'm not discounting any cancers, life-threatening diseases or rare ones that people have faced or battled. I'm truly grateful for those I met along the way and for all who helped make our lives better daily. Those who have heard the words "cancer" and "incurable" in the same sentence know what I mean. It puts just about anyone in the fight or flight mode. We chose to fight when Michael was diagnosed in September 2017. What was worse, was my brother and sister-in-law were also diagnosed with different cancers at the same time. That was a month to remember. A year to reflect on.

I admit, I'm a pretty salty-mouthed person with a not-too-great filter. Yet, I dislike the #fcancer signs, shirts and so forth. You would think I would be the perfect person to represent this, having three of my family members diagnosed. It's actually the opposite. It's not offensive, but I also won't give cancer that much power. I didn't feel that would be what defines us and who we were as a family or anyone who fights cancer.

We went through standard care which was radiation and a chemo pill. Giving someone a chemo pill is really strange, knowing what it does to a person. The fact that he was never sick and was just tired from it, was fortunate for us. We finished days before Christmas, watching him ring the final bell that signaled the end of radiation treatments. It was a holiday of mixed emotions, but we were together and that was everything. Family memories mattered and we made the most of it, not knowing if it was the last one we would celebrate as a family of three. We had a month of waiting to see how the treatment and surgery worked.

January came and the MRI told our fate like a fortune teller with a crystal ball. We had no thought to be afraid because he had done so well through it. In fact, he was biking and walking to work. The surgery had been successful with a total removal. We went that day, had the test and went straight to the doctor for the results. We walked in as he put up the scans. It really didn't take a brain surgeon (pun intended) to look at the scan to know it was bad, really bad. The doctor's face showed it all, completely blindsided. I put on my best game face that I could muster. Trying not to show utter devastation at this point was the only option. It was full Virago that day until I went to bed after telling his family the news that it had gone from fully removed to tripling in size.

When I think back now, it felt like anytime I thought it wasn't good news, I put that toward being stronger, not weaker. I'll never forget when our son Cole took him for his MRI the day before the next surgery, where they put markers on for the surgical team. I was at work while Cole was filling out the medical form. Oh good grief, please let your teens start filling out forms. He called me asking if he had a metal plate (FYI he did and I had no idea after the first surgery) and when his last period was. I was pretty sure he could answer the last one! And, mind you, I was at the salon with a customer who was now laughing as well. Last question, he wasn't sure about an IUD, "Isn't that what blows up?" he asked. I love that boy with everything I have. I tried explaining to him that no, that's an IED. He did have it somewhat correct, because if it did fail, it would have had the person "blow up" in another way. Yes, we have a weird sense of humor. I'm not apologizing and if you laughed, you are my kind of people!

They got home *way* later than I could imagine. It never took that long, but Cole said they had to do it all over again. Michael was moving and wanted Cole close by. It was strange because he usually did the test with no problem. This time, however, he could barely get out of the car. He was acting very spacey, almost like someone on an acid trip, staring at strange things. I called the doctor immediately, he gave me the okay to give him a few more of one medication. I handed him his normal batch, and when I turned my back briefly with the doctor still on the phone, all of a sudden I could hear him not choking, but chewing his meds! That poor doctor had never heard me blurt out colorful words like that! At that point, he asked if he should call an ambulance or could I drive him. Mind you, it took us 20 minutes to get him out of the car. This time, though, it took us no time at all and half the time to get to the hospital. They were waiting and couldn't get him out when we finally arrived! I believe he chewed those pills and the reason was simple, if he hadn't, I really think he wouldn't have made it. He was ready to go into massive seizures. It wasn't his time; we were to still have more time with him. We got to fight that fight; we were fortunate. That week was all about keeping calm, and the game plan had changed drastically. Have you seen that life plan drawing, where it's straight as an arrow, always straight up to the top, but in reality, it's a squirrelly mess? That was us, that mess! But we were a mess together. It was survival mode, quality of life and making every moment count.

Meanwhile, both my brother-in-law and sister-in-law had their second surgeries, and all went well. We needed good news in this family. While this was all happening, working full time on my nail and jewelry business. Michael thought it was funny when he first went to the hospital – I had been recognized and promoted that same month from the jewelry company. He was always my biggest fan. Support systems and people are just as important as food and water. My nail customers and salon family are extremely supportive. I'm so thankful I'm with a company that makes me stretch my giving side. It has helped me grow in more ways than I could imagine. To seek ways to help others and have more of a grateful heart with an outlet to get out of my head makes a difference. That has come back to me tenfold. I tightened up my salon schedule, gave events to my jewelry designers and only did a select few. I took Michael with me as much as possible. We made time together as good as it could be, even when he had the few chemotherapy infusions. I got him his favorite strawberry shakes for the short infusions that lasted 4-6 hours. When we knew this was the fight of his life, we also went into alternative methods. I have to thank my sister-in-law who is a tenacious Google fiend.

Did you ever wonder about that saying, "Everything happens for a reason?" Not cancer, but going places, seeing old friends or meeting people along the way? There is a reason, a lesson to be learned or reminder that you are not alone. We were at a birthday party just months before his diagnosis and met our friend who we hadn't been in contact with for years. It felt like we hadn't even missed a beat! Jenny had been working in the medical profession and transitioned into helping others with cannabis products. Never miss an opportunity to grow and learn new things; I have no regrets to opening new doors in my life. I always say I have "cat lives" because I have had unique opportunities and experiences. You can choose to have control, lose it or go full throttle. With any life-threatening disease, you learn that the only thing you have true control over is how you react to it. I chose to be positive and to all I met, as open as I could be to learning more, being mindful of others along the way. Don't ever beat yourself up over what you should have done or said, it's okay. Forgive that person you were and learn that lesson. You are stronger than you think.

I am grateful for everyone we came in contact with, for what we had, our travels and our lives. We truly lived with no regrets; we didn't wait until we were retired to travel and do things, we did them. Don't learn that the hard way; we are here on this earth for a short time. For those of us who found our soulmates, you probably have a picture in your head of the two of you old and grey in a rocking chair, finally enjoying that sunrise or sunset. STOP!!! Enjoy it NOW! I was that person who thought Michael would outlive me; it made sense because he was eight years younger. Where was my reality check? I came to the realization that it wasn't about him spending the rest of our lives together, but it was to have spent the rest of his life with me. Gratitude is everything. We were and are fortunate that everything happened when it did. Our son Cole was getting his career started and Michael got to see that. I'm not saying there won't moments where you break down and sob, cry or just have that feeling of utter devastation. You are going to have them, but it's how you work or deal with them that will help you move forward.

That September was hell for us, or so I thought. In an emergency, I try to slow everything down, breathe, focus (for a Gemini that is an accomplishment) and get into that Virago-mode. Maintaining a positive attitude is everything; it helps everyone! It's not easy to do at times; think of being prepared for a disaster when it happens. You practice it, you know what you would do and when it happens you do it. It's the same, you can try to be prepared for anything, even when hearing devastating news you can use those tools. You need to feed your soul and your deep inner energy levels. Don't ignore those, you need to be able to use those sometimes for long periods of times. What re-energizes you? Sleep, going to the beach, the sun, deep breathing, meditation, music? Do what works for you to give you that positive vibe. You can't help anyone when you are empty. I talk to myself either out loud or through my inner voice. How do you speak to yourself? Are you harder? Kinder? A cheerleader? Practice good, kinder words.

You are amazing, look at what you have gone through! If you are constantly bullying yourself, what are you projecting? You are worth the effort. Don't be afraid to ask for help if you can't get out of it. I had some amazing help that we surrounded ourselves with. It's necessary to have that, and if you're a control freak, that is something you need to let go of quickly. Take those warm hugs and have people that make you laugh and feel safe around you more often. Smiling and laughing is so important, it's the best for everyone. My son Cole and I have a pretty crazy relationship, we laugh at the strangest things. I'm grateful daily for those laughs. We all have bad moments, that's normal, but it's how we get through them that is important. Take the time to figure out which tools will help you. I used music the most; going to my events was a way to help others as my tool to realign my strength. Some days my music was heavy metal when I felt I needed more strength, but most of the time it was pure happy music that made me smile. Going to work was a good diversion, I never let my customers know how bad it was because they already had their own shit to deal with, so why pour my crazy life into theirs? Did I post it on social media? No! I did, however, add a group page that kept our friends and family more informed. That was a good way to keep it real and positive for us as well. It was a good way to let others send their prayers, good vibes and thoughts to us, which were always welcomed.

September 2018 we went camping, something we loved to do year-round. But this time it was special. He was doing pretty well, but definitely wasn't at his best. Learn the lesson that every day you are on this earth, you are making a memory for someone or something. Memories are what we have left when someone is gone, good or bad. Get into that positive mindset to make good memories in the face of absolute hell. Camping was actually really great because we were surrounded by friends and family. Later that month, we went to a celebration of life for one of his high school friends. He would have turned fifty that day.

Many of his friends were there. Michael had his ups and downs but looked great. His memory from the last surgery wasn't good, it was like being with an Alzheimer's patient at times. He was battling an infection which was soon to be what he lost the fight to. He loved seeing his friends and had the best day seeing them, as well as them seeing him. It was a moment to take note that I would be doing this for him in the future.

He went in for surgery yet again, this time for the infection. I wasn't worried at all, but that's when we got word that his battle was coming to an end. How do you prepare a family for this? We knew time wasn't on our side, but now? I had never been so proud to see Cole at the young age of twenty step up and talk to the rest of our family. We were always told to hope for the best but prepare for the worst. It was time to prepare and tell them the worst news possible. To prepare his family for the fact that his father had weeks left on this earth. Cole is truly the best of both of us, and it was time to think about facing a life without Michael by our sides. It was time for Michael to live out his remaining days surrounded by friends and family he loved and making the most of every day. He needed care and thanks to Jenny, we had that! She made him laugh and we were able to make the best of a bad situation.

With Thanksgiving just around the corner, we knew it was going to be a big outing. It wasn't easy getting him ready and out of the house, but we did it. He was full of life that day; he put every bit of energy he had into it. He was so excited to hear our niece announce that she was going to have her first baby. He got to be part of that news, and that was a huge reality moment. Michael loved his nieces with everything he had. He was their "Funcle" and they loved him. It was probably one of the first times I really wanted to escape and just give in to that moment of heartache for everyone. I was so excited for them as well, but deep in my core was that harsh reality that he would be gone. He was wiped out, and that day was his last day to be okay. His decline was noticeable. He was losing the battle and even the hospice nurse was shocked that it was so rapid. It was true, he was good until he wasn't, he was done fighting. It was time to let go. This is probably the hardest thing you will ever face in your life. Losing a parent is hard. Losing the person you chose to live out your days with is harder. It's also freeing to those who have been in that position. We all got to say how much he meant to us, he had fought the fight and was surrounded by his family and friends when his brave spirit left us that day. It was a love-filled room and a peaceful transition.

Lives change in an instant, and for us it was September 2017. To live life, you need to be okay with any change in a moment. As I write this story of love, strength and inspiration, it's been six months since my new normal began. Do I miss Michael? Hell yes! Everyone will tell you it's a year of change. I see that but know that it is actually a lifetime of change. Not bad, just different. Valentine's Day was tough because we had met on that night. Remember that celebration of life? We had it and it was epic! It was mostly for his family to show he was beloved by so many. It was also a healing process for them and his friends to remember him and heal. Not to move on, but forward. It was important to be mindful of his dad to let him see how much his son had accomplished and whose lives he had touched. It's important to celebrate birthdays even more to me now.

Having gratitude in my life makes it easier to be a more positive person. I find that by helping others, it helps me and in turn gives me endless happiness. I'm outgoing and energetic, but also an ambivert at heart. At times I need to get away or be by myself to recharge my warrior spirit.

So change that music playlist, look in the mirror and laugh out loud. You deserve happiness. Look for positive people and groups that make you happy and feel needed. Put yourself out into the universe and say, "I'm worth it." I know Michael, my biggest fan, is right there, laughing that nothing can stop me. I'm not afraid to think about the future because his memory and our memories of him won't go away. I'll have new memories and new adventures. Face the day with everything you got. No one else is going to live it for you. Be a Virago Spirit!

KANDICE'S INSPIRATION TIPS

Never discount how much inner strength you really have.

People don't move on, they move forward with their lives.

Be aware of low energy/vampires who can suck the life out of you. Limit their time.

Take time to re-energize yourself from time to time. Self-care is key.

Make a happy playlist of songs.

Take help and hugs when you can.

Kandice Astamendi is a 40 year veteran in the beauty industry, both behind the chair and as a consultant/educator for several manufacturers. She was named American Business Women's Woman of the Year and was the Way and Means Chair for four years. Recognized from *Business Life Magazine* one of their Women of Achievement in 2019. Kandice currently runs her own nail business and consults for an international nail company. For the past three years she has been with Origami Owl customizable jewelry and one of the top in sales since joining.

Connect with Kandice
www.Kandice98.OrigamiOwl.com

Magical things happen when you **ACTIVATE** YOUR FAITH.

~ Susie Augustin

From The Ashes To a Healthy Mind, Body & Soul

by Lisa Giannini

Educated in westernized medicine, I would never disfavor the throngs of medical treatment available for someone in crisis. However, in hindsight, my rise from the ashes of dancing with the devil in darkness for many years came not just from a rebalancing of brain neurochemistry, but also from learning to gracefully retrain and heal my mind. It was progress not perfection, practicing mindfulness, slowing thoughts and learning to separate thoughts from feelings.

The darkest days of depression is a level of despair that is so heavy, so empty and so deep, this feels like a black hole of abyss. Unless one has experienced it, quite frankly, it is difficult to describe the utter pain of emotional anguish. It numbs your core and keeps you void of feeling alive and normal. Anxiety, on the other hand, chokes you. We have all experienced a limb falling asleep and that eerie pins-and-needles tingling that masks the normal sensation. Now imagine that sensation occurring on your insides from the very top of your head to the absolute tips of your toes, with no way to massage it out to relieve that creepy feeling. It is like an internal frayed wire that keeps misfiring but the wire is the body's own electrical circuit. Your nervous system is going haywire. As the system keeps firing in a continuous state of fight or flight, you feel like you struggle to catch your breath and are suffocating. Panic takes over. There is a heavy weight in your chest, your mind begins to race and you want to jump out of your own skin because you feel like if it does not stop, you just might actually die.

This is my personal experience with depression and anxiety. As if the combination of choking desperation is not awful enough, what is worse is that while your body's insides are in absolute disequilibrium, your outside appears quite normal. Anyone near you may consider you a complete lunatic because nothing "appears" to actually be wrong. Therein lies the shame of both major depressive disorder and generalized anxiety disorder. The painful anguish, fear, and dark cloud of despair lingers when everyone else seems to be smiling and going about their business, all while you silently suffer. It's truly enough for one to want to break through to the other side. The moments your internal body is not at war with itself is fleeting and daily chores of life become unconquerable mountains. Life's joys are anesthetized, you fake it until you make it and otherwise benign stressors put you completely over the edge. Devoid of light and hope, the intricate roller coaster of this inner world of dark fear and adrenaline, followed by exhausted surge depletion, is a ride people are opting off of and instead hitting the ejector seat.

Initial stages of healing my mind required rediscovering my creative side and finding activities that generated calmer feelings and peace. I learned to tap into those activities to slow down triggering and racing thoughts. Certain scents, textures and colors further helped soothe my system, and in discovering which ones helped, I adopted them into routine activities of daily life. I used a timer to literally give myself a time-out when my physical body would rebel, I practiced grounding and visualized the formation of new neural pathways firing in my brain. It was repeatedly difficult to actually believe that the practice of any of it would ever bring a full feeling of light and essence back to my soul, but since I remained alive, I was determined to make sense of the diagnosis and passionate about seeking complete wellness. Feeling sick and dying had already robbed me of too many years.

While the better part of two years was spent practicing these life-changing and life-saving skills, I could not help but still feel something was wrong. Or more so, something was not well. My progress was reinforced in the medical community but inadvertently I felt medicated, bloated, had decreased energy and felt toxic. I was alive and living, but wasn't convinced that this was what "being well" was supposed to feel like. Lackluster health was not acceptable, as it left a vague dimness around me that felt too reminiscent of the rabbit hole I was trying to crawl out from. Always the caregiver, I did not practice worthy self-care and had an "aha" moment when I realized that if I wanted more out of this healing journey, it was up to me to keep pushing forward. The thought occurred to me, "If I change what I put in my body, could I change my body chemistry?" After all, the body is a machine and what goes in it affects how it operates. It baffled me that no one had thought of this sooner. Just as I had to take accountability for practicing my own mind's healing, I took accountability for practicing better body health. I have always enjoyed exercise and did not see myself as a horrific eater, but I did not realize the profound affects unconscious consumption has on overall wellness.

Ironically, and what I believe to be divine coincidence, I had discovered a program designed to nutritionally detoxify the body that would help me test my theory. Physiologically, the body is designed to maintain homeostasis, or to maintain its own internal stability. The body's parts want to work together to respond to disturbances that disrupt normal function. With my instincts telling me this would lead to other answers for the wellness I sought, I jumped in with full force. I needed an alternative way to further reset my out of sync chemistry. While the human body is wondrous in how much it can adapt, it too has tipping points. With the same meticulousness with which I was forced to practice mental healing, I invested time piecing together the problems with the fuel that was, or rather was not, nourishing my body. With so much chronic illness in western culture, I put my thinking cap on and started adjusting other puzzle pieces.

A large majority of the western diet is made up of processed foods containing artificial sweeteners, chemicals and preservatives. Natural foods like fruits and vegetables are genetically modified, artificially altered and are sprayed with herbicides and pesticides. This has become the accepted norm for food, and while these things have been made edible for human consumption, the list of chemicals could not possibly be helpful in reclaiming anyone's wellness. In fact, I was the naïve person who did not spend much time reading package ingredients, because not only was the verbiage inconceivable to pronounce, but who has the time to spend figuring out what all those chemical ingredients mean? That is exactly where the buck stopped. If I did not know what those man-made ingredients manufactured in a chemist's lab were, how did I expect my body's organs to know what they were or what to do with them? How was this affecting my neurochemistry, and was it sabotaging my healing despite my best efforts? Inadvertently, I started eliminating processed, allergenic and inflammatory foods and began replacing them with cleaner versions. I paid attention to ingredient listings and kept it simple. If I could recognize what the listed ingredients were, then essentially, my body could too. I incorporated nutrient-dense food and supplements and gave my liver, kidneys and digestive tract a reprieve from having to filter and sort synthesized junk. With my body's filtration and reabsorption systems less inundated with unrecognizable synthetics, it was instead flooded with nutrient-dense and high vibrational food full of the earth's natural life force energy. I was not only speaking a newly learned language to my mind, but also to my body's other organs via quality medicine in the form of real God-given food.

So, how did I come to begin healing my soul? When you are depressed and anxious, no one tells you when the light is going to come back. There is no protocol to follow guaranteeing its return, but the grievous irony is that is exactly what you crave. The pathway is a road of trial and action to customize the route back to the light of your soul. Once I learned to manage my mind and cleaned up my machine, my unrelenting quest to seek more answers led me to my deepest work in personal growth. I, once upon a time, never thought my soul would see the light of day again, so when the light began to return in tiny shimmering glimpses, I wanted to learn whatever it took to stay there. My passionate drive of determination came not just because I wanted to chase the light, but rather to distance myself far from the bleak painful darkness that had shrouded so much of my experience for years.

In the perplexity of depression and anxiety, you scream to be out of your own body. From this point of view, the idea of becoming one with yourself and being aligned internally seems like the most absurd thing on the planet. You may even ask, "What is that? Is it fathomable when it feels like your internal norm is total chaos?" The concept of oneness where the soul is concerned is quite literal. Once familiarized with the practices of yoga, meditation and basic teachings of great masters of peace, there is a repeating underlying theme about finding peace within. It is learning to become so calm and serene that you find the hidden oasis in your own heart and soul center. That becomes the foundation from which you start to begin to live and view others. I had no checklist to start from in this part of my recovery, or rather what I call my rediscovery, but there is nothing more empowering than knowing there is a hard-reset button of healing within a peaceful place in my heart. So many times, I prayed to be relieved of the pain that no one could see as I reached for the hem of His garment for a way out. I begged on my hands and knees, vulnerable and stripped naked, that if I was just shown the way, I promised I would begin to follow.

When we are born, our soul is not conditioned to blame or criticize imperfections, and we do not focus on trying to impress others. We are complete as we are because nothing has conditioned us otherwise. Innately, the human spirit has a deep desire to be coupled with others and feel deeply connected and understood. It actually becomes the foundation of sound mind we seek, therefore not having to prove ourselves to anyone or to ourselves that we are enough. We learn to fear failure, compete against others to elevate ourselves and to chase after material needs for fulfillment. When fear, competition and materialism become thoughtless habitual patterns we use to glorify ourselves, we end up on a path of misguided focus, straying further and further from the soul from which we began. It is no wonder people find themselves lost and unhappy. This pattern coupled with depression and anxiety that biologically clouds the mind and misfires the neurological system, are perfectly measured ingredients for a recipe of dark disaster.

Only through removing each veil and healing both mind and body could I begin to understand oneness and how returning to the soul, our original essence, is where I would find completely aligned wholeness. In fact, it is our soul, the internal guidance system, which is the true on-demand driver of our lives. With authentic intention to multiply healing and understanding, I share my truth in finding a healthy life in mind, body and soul for the next one of my soul brothers or sisters who suffers and may be wandering, lost in the dark. With humble, gentle kindness, open mindedness, love and understanding, all of us should strive to not only look out for ourselves, but to look out for the collective wellness of all human kind so that everyone learns to practice illuminating the dark and shining a brighter light on higher consciousness. With an open heart and courage to be vulnerable, I only hope my experience plants seeds from which a tree of healing and enlightenment can sprout from one another. Where there is light, there is love, and where there is love, there is an awakening for us all.

LISA'S MIND BODY SOUL TIPS

- Mindfulness – It is more effective to do one thing at a time. Remain present in the moment to discover your inner oasis.

- Personal Growth – By beginning to transform ourselves, we can begin to transform our circumstances.

- Food is Medicine – Eat wisely. The body regenerates itself. With every bite we take, we participate in the recreation of a new version of ourselves.

- Love is Always the Answer – By making choices from a place of love (what we love doing, who we love spending time with), we no longer imprison our soul.

- We Are Sixth Sensory Beings – Listen to your "gut instinct." It is the link to the guidance system driving our lives.

- Selfish Isn't Selfish – Provide self-care to your most intimate companion, you. Harness enough life force energy so that there is enough to give a percentage away to others.

Lisa Giannini, MSN, RNC, NP, has 20+ years of experience in the medical, health and wellness field. She's practiced at a world-renowned medical center, is an AFAA Certified Fitness Instructor, and has studied mind-body healing arts and chakra balancing. An intuitive empath passionate about mind-body healing, Lisa operates a consulting business coaching others to discover a healthy life from the inside out. When not on the wellness road, Lisa spends time with her only child (a rescue dog), dancing, and living her best life with loved ones.

Connect with Lisa
LisaGiannini.com • IG @LisagLifeisGood

REFLECTIONS

by Xiomara Escobar

I can remember the clinking of champagne, celebrating our teams' success in my Pink career with Mary Kay. After some tough years in starting a small business, I had now closed back to back years of hitting our sales goals. I was envisioning my new Pink year with all the new endeavors. Being an entrepreneur has not been an easy feat, but what I built there allows me to have my most proud moments. It allows me to work with amazing women and I get to teach and serve my clients in their beauty needs. I had no idea that for the next two years, because of family circumstances, I wouldn't work my business the way I had in the past. There was no way to prepare for the "surprises" around the corner.

White never seemed so devastating a color while listening to the deafening sound of a pen tapping against the clipboard. It was as though someone had punched me in my stomach and had pulled my heart out, but still wanted me to respond to the news that was just delivered to me. The oncologist was telling me that my father's colon cancer was stage 4, which meant that it had spread all over his body. The mass in his colon was growing so fast that he had only six months to live. My father was in the other room and didn't know what we were discussing, so I later told my parents it was about the medical insurance. I remember so vividly kissing my parents goodbye after the doctor's appointment and sitting in the parking lot for 30 minutes sobbing. How was I supposed to respond to the news? Should I start planning my father's funeral, and how could I possibly tell my mom this news? All I remember is that I got a call from my best friend and thinking, "Well, life goes on," and headed to my next destination. Being able to compartmentalize is one of my talents that at this moment I had to implement. I had no idea I would have to use that muscle a lot.

I dreaded having to call my insurance agent and make sure my mom would be okay and create a plan. That particular day I had a breakdown and started to cry with such intensity it hurt my whole being. I sat there thinking that if I told my father, I would bring him into a depression and I didn't want him to lose faith and hope, even though I was feeling numb inside.

Monday came strolling around and it was our first day at chemotherapy at the Hoag Cancer Center in Irvine, California. We had no idea what to expect, except the week prior we were made aware that the chemo would be three consecutive days and we would be coming to Hoag for the chemotherapy sessions. I remember I passed many walls but didn't take the time to notice anything on them. As we exited, I noticed one of the walls had these words of affirmations, but one word stuck out to me, "faith." I thought it was nice for families that had hope to activate their faith, but I simply felt sad and numb. I just sighed, walked away and was impressed with the wall, but didn't think I could ever be motivated by the wall, as my father had such a dire predicament, or so I thought.

Our first surgery had arrived and we had no idea yet again what to expect. It's what needed to be done, as my father's health and body was dilapidating. My father had reached 114 pounds, which became evident even more when we as a family went to Disneyland. We took a picture and he was so excited to be at the happiest place on earth, but sat down on benches to take a breath throughout the whole trip. I remember keeping it together, but at night I cried with my husband as I knew the surgery was our only way to a better situation for my father. At this point he was in severe pain with abdominal bloating from being unable to defecate normally due to his colon failing. I remember getting anxious phone calls from my mom, worried that it was day three and he still hadn't defecated. The surgery was a success because we were told that my dad would have a bag for more than likely all his life. Dr. Bui was able to make a clean cut of the colon tumor and there was no need for the bag. Of course, my brother had to tell my father as he was waking up that the bag was huge, and I of course had to intercede and be like, "No Dad, there is no bag." Some laughter among the tension around the current circumstance was good. We had survived our first round of chemotherapy and our first surgery in Newport Beach Hoag Hospital in the books.

After that, I walked through the Hoag Cancer Center and looked at the wall with hope, joy and a faith that started sparkling. At that moment, I surrendered my wishes and allowed God to work through me. I knew as a family we had a tough and unknown road ahead, but I knew I had to let go of the uncertainty and fear and just know that God had full control of it all. As I walked through our first doctor's appointment with our oncologist, I had no idea we would have an intense conversation with my dad as he started started getting very temperamental and extremely agitated with everyone. Falling into a depression, even though we had our win, the cancer cell count had only dropped 200 points, so my father thought he had sacrificed himself and now he had this big scar on his belly from this first surgery. My father became defiant and didn't want to follow the protocol that the doctor was suggesting or take more chemotherapy sessions. I was very upset because I had allowed my father to waste a year on alternative therapies that didn't work, so this time around I would take control. My father stormed out of the room and broke my heart and my mother's. Disappointment was evident and hurt to my core. A couple of hours later my father called me and said he would proceed with the protocol the doctor had laid out. Yep, you guessed it, I cried fountains of tears of joy and anger.

The summer of 2017, I was at one of my networking events and got the news right before I started the event that I was hosting that we had to bring my father to the hospital because a fatal bacteria was affecting him. Since the show must go on, I went through with the event. Immediately after, I ran over to the hospital for my father's emergency surgery, which a plastic surgeon had to treat. It was extremely frustrating as for almost a day, no one could decide which surgeon would take care of this odd bacteria growing in his chest and by his nipple.

I prayed with such intensity and passion and gave up on

trying to find the solution to the problems and situation that lay ahead. For two and a half years, we fought the battle with three surgeries. My dad reached his last chemo in May 2019; he defied every single odd and the doctors said they had only read about miracles, but never actually witnessed them. I knew it wasn't fate and good luck, but it was my dad's purpose to minister to others that are going through cancer, to fight like Rocky Balboa.

My Heavenly Father, my Lord and Savior, holds all of the beauty and praise for the Miracle he did on my father. My faith in my Lord Jesus was the strong foundation in which I laid my prayers at his feet. It took courage and tenacity to look up, even when I thought my dad wouldn't see the light of day. That's why I give thanks to my God for giving me another day to live on this earth to serve Him and his people.

This cancer experience with my father has shaped me into a woman of strength and endurance, and an abundance of patience beyond what I ever imagined. Now as I look to return to my dedication and support to our Pink Team and to being a female entreprenuer, I am ready for all challenges that may come. I am full of courage and writing has become to me, empowering, where I can express my emotions and journey throughout my experiences. Come follow me through my blog! Traveling around the globe to enrich my soul and traveling throughout the states to empower other women to find their inner beauty through the vehicle of Mary Kay. Confidence is the best makeup you will ever wear! Muah!

XIOMARA'S WARRIOR TIPS

🎤 It's okay that you don't have all the answers.

🎤 Be present with those you love and care about.

🎤 Be confident. It's the best makeup tip I can ever give a woman!

🎤 Know that you are not in control of everything, but a higher being is always there and you can reach Him through prayer and faith.

🎤 Acknowledge your emotions even if it's sadness or fear. Do not marinate in negative feelings but acknowledge its presence and let go. Your soul will thank you!

🎤 Strength is found inside each one of us.

🎤 LOVE with all your heart.

🎤 Sparkle in your own way.

Xiomara Escobar is The CEO and founder of her own unique beauty business and mission, with a passion to enrich women's lives, helping them radiate out positive energy and encouraging them to discover their own beauty and self love from the inside out. As a motivational speaker, her belief is that confidence is the best makeup a woman can ever wear, and she walks this talk radiating out positivity and kindness. Xiomara has supported numerous non-profit organizations as well as led and planned fundraising events all over Southern California. She has been volunteering for the Casa Teresa domestic violence shelter for over eight years. She is currently the Inner Beauty Queen for Love Thy Neighbor.

Connect with Xiomara
www.TheDivaWearsPink.com • IG @TheDivaWearsPink

A Gift From Above

by Harriette Tapia

I am a woman that may come off as a little shy and reserved to people who don't know me. However, I have a lot to say when given the chance. I am a very caring, loving and patient mother, grandmother and friend! I am quick witted and love to laugh, which is one of the reasons why my boyfriend and I have been together for 28 years.

In my forties, I was told I had a tumor in my right breast, which was labeled as noninvasive cancer. What are you talking about? Cancer does not run in my family! Only heart disease and insanity runs in the family, so how can that be? I had a few biopsies done from that same breast in the past, and each time they came out clean. The surgeon said the positive thing was that it was the smallest amount of cancer he had seen in years, and we caught it about eight years before it would turn into a tumor. He wanted to go back and make sure he had gotten all of it. Everything came back clean.

So now what do I do? They said it was really up to me because it was such a small amount. I made an appointment with a radiologist for treatment options. "Radiation." This was not easy for me to hear since I had been doing more natural protocols and didn't have any other symptoms. The radiologist explained that I would be going five days a week for a number of weeks. By doing the radiation, the chances of the cancer returning would be cut by 90%. That wasn't so bad!

As I was lying on a cold table looking up at the nurse making marks on my body, she quickly explained the treatments and finished up. It's often said that there is a message to learn when you go through an illness like cancer. I tried to figure out what my message was for years and spoke to the other patients to see if they knew what their message was. Some did and some didn't.

I have always wanted to help people. When I was working

in the weight loss industry, I received that chance, however I knew I was meant to help people on a larger scale. It took me some time, but I finally found my message. I have always had two passions in life, helping people and health. When I was introduced to The Emotion Code Protocol, I realized I had found my calling!

The Emotion Code is powerful energy healing. By tapping into your own subconscious mind, you are able to identify stored energy from an old emotional trauma and release it in seconds. The beauty of this protocol is you do not have to relive that trauma again.

You don't even have to talk about it. Your subconscious mind is like your own computer. It holds the key to your well-being.

I am a certified practitioner in The Emotion Code by Dr. Bradley Nelson. With Dr. Nelson's guidance and The Emotion Code chart, you are able to identify from 60 different emotions that may be trapped. These 60 emotions cover hundreds if not thousands of emotions.

If we don't process the emotion from events it can then become a trapped energy in your body. These trapped emotions can fester in your life and body, creating pain, malfunction, and eventual disease. With this protocol you are also able to identify prenatal and inherited trapped emotions as well. All of these can cause an emotional and physical toll on you. One of the most damaging of all, trapped emotions that gather around your heart. This is called a heart wall which can interfere with your ability to give and receive love.

Emotions can impact the level of success and abundance you are able to achieve. We are driven by our emotions, and now I help release trapped emotions so you can have abundant health, love and happiness! I am in love with what I do!

HARRIETTE'S INSPIRATION TIPS

SUCCESS comes in all shapes and sizes. Break up your to do list so it isn't so overwhelming. Have an accountability person. Keep picking yourself up after you have fallen, and continue to move forward. Believe in yourself and your value. Your success will continue to rise to the top!

CONFIDENCE – With each decade of life comes growth. The more we face our fears and insecurities, the more confident we become. We all have gifts, so own it! Know that you don't have to defend your actions at all times. Know that by accomplishing something small, you will be able to accomplish something on an even larger scale.

INSPIRATION – You can be inspired by a person, place or experience. Don't give up trying to do what you truly desire. Keep searching for what will continue to bring you inspiration. Sometimes you don't have to look very far because you could be the one that brings inspiration to someone else. If you are so blessed to inspire someone, in return you will be inspired as well!

Harriette Tapia is an experienced healer, driven by her passion to provide the best experience possible for her clients. She has worked in the health industry for over 20 years and helps her clients with weight loss. As a certified practitioner in The Emotion Code, her goals include building a rapport with her clients so together they can identify and release trapped emotions, which creates healing. In addition to her main functions as a practitioner, Harriette has been recognized by her clients for her compassion and commitment to their health goals. She is also certified in behavior modification and has worked with clients 1:1 and in group settings, for over 16 years. She loves going up to her cabin in the mountains with her family and friends.

Connect with Harriette
www.Harrieshealthyhaven.com
FB Harries Healthy Haven • IG @HarrietteTapia88

CONFIDENCE

The Dalai Lama said, "Calm mind brings inner strength and self-confidence, so that's very important for good health." The good news is that confidence can be learned. It can be developed. Even if you had a childhood filled with negative experiences, or have had some challenges as an adult, you can transform that into wisdom and bring on the confidence.

When you feel deep passion about your purpose, are clear about your path, set and achieve goals, have the courage to believe in yourself and your dreams, you will feel confident. You will feel enthusiastic and assertive, inspiring others. Does this mean that you need to have a huge purpose, wanting to save the world and change the lives of millions? No. Your purpose may be to be in a great relationship and be a wonderful mom, and in doing so, others might come to you for relationship advice and you'll be known as the neighborhood kids' "second mom." You can go big and start your own non-profit to help others. Your self-confidence and optimism will motivate others to have the courage to explore and design their own journey.

When you use your imagination and determination to pursue your goals, big or small, you help others do the same. Confidence and forward thinking creates opportunities to help you live the life you desire.

A huge way to step into confidence is to try new things, travel, have 20 seconds of courage and just do things you're afraid of. Don't compare yourself to others, know that you deserve greatness, change up your routines, see yourself through the eyes of those who love you, and dare to own who you are, your story and your purpose, no matter how unique it may be. That is true confidence.

WHEN YOUR LIFE PURPOSE CHANGES

by Anita Salazar

Aloha. I fell in love with Maui 37 years ago on my honeymoon. It wasn't just the beautiful Island but their Aloha spirit, spiritual connections and ability to get refreshed. We tried to figure out a way to move there but our circumstances didn't allow it. So we decided that if we couldn't move there we would make it our mission to go every year. So we did and it became "our island."

When I get off the plane at the airport in Maui, the humidity hits me and I am home. My "hale" is here. I feel like I am alive again. Sometimes we do nothing but go to the beach every day, lay under the umbrella and watch the waves, sit on the lanai and relax or read. We drive around the island and enjoy the energy it gives. There is so much Aloha energy there. The ocean, the sand, the sea turtles. I need to have water in my life. Because the water has such a life force, and the power of it brings me happiness.

A few years ago, at age 50, I started searching for myself – I felt like I was done with life. My purpose from when I was a child was always – be a mom, be a wife. I did it, I have two daughters and helped raise three grandkids, and I threw a career in the mix. Grandkids are now in preschool, I don't have to work at the family business, and now I didn't have a purpose – I felt there was pressure from everyone that I was supposed to have some grand purpose. I didn't know what I was supposed to do. My confidence hit an all-time low.

I met Kim Somers Egelsee through Kyle Wilson. I decided to join Kim's confidence course and then her mastermind, which was not an easy thing to do. This was completely out of my comfort zone. After my first mastermind and realizing that during this time my purpose is ME, I was surprised that I was okay with this.

Once I got my inner confidence, everything in my life started to move forward and change. I discovered inner happiness by starting to do the things that I wanted to do, rather than sitting back and being the wallflower, or staying stuck in what everyone expected me to do. I started to put myself as a priority with self-love, self-care and self-help. I realized that I am valued and stopped the inner judging voice. This felt great! I discovered the "me" I was always meant to be. Most of my family and friends embraced the new me and were shocked that I didn't already have the inner confidence, since I've always portrayed it. I had outer confidence, but not inner confidence. Inner confidence helped me discover my purpose and helped with my relationships because I was starting to stand up for what I believe. This has brought me into my spiritual path. I have also experienced positive changes in my overall health, as I added in healthy habits and honored my body and its limitations, I was able to put my conditions into remission (fibromyalgia, chronic fatigue, Epstein-Barr). I am able to do more and be more present since I am no longer fighting off the pain, fatigue, brain fog and depression. I was able to start a new career of travel with The Real Estate Guys Radio Event Team. With my new confidence and believing in my own power, I am able to make decisions that I would have never been able to before. I am realizing who I am, and this has made me a stronger person.

My purpose is to be the best me that I am! I love to travel to Maui, live my life, help my family, and just be present. Hitting my all-time low gave me the gift of finding myself loved, honored, cherished and liked by the most influential person in my life. ME! Once I did that, I am now capable of doing other stuff. For example, now when I introduce myself, I come from confidence and don't minimize what I do. Now I get to be who I'm supposed to be in my life.

ANITA'S CONFIDENCE TIPS

🎤 Embrace yourself.

🎤 Invest in your healing, energy and spirituality.

🎤 Step into your life with confidence...even if it means just being YOU!

🎤 Life is like a wave – you have to just go with the flow. Sometimes that wave can crush you, but you can just stand up and shake it off.

🎤 Enjoy your life.

🎤 Get out of your comfort zone, you never know what amazing things will happen.

Anita Salazar is a wife, mom and Mor~Mor (grandmother). She runs a family corporation and is part of the The Real Estate Guys Radio Event Team, traveling and putting on events for 200+ across the country. In her downtime she loves spending time with her husband Reuben. Anita loves to travel and her favorite destination is Maui, where the magical islands are like home to her.

Connect with Anita
IG @EnchantingAnita

Follow
YOUR
PASSION!
SEE AND
EXPERIENCE
JOY.

~ Kim Somers Egelsee

IF I CAN, YOU CAN

by Melissa Tori

Two-ton Tori...It can run. Two-ton Tori...It can run. Those were the chants my classmates shouted as I ran in PE in the sixth grade. I still remember the person's name that started it all.

I was an emotional eater most of my life. Eating was how I dealt with life. I ate for comfort.

On December 26, 2014, I hit rock bottom. I was sitting on the couch watching TV alone at 10:30 in the morning with a half-gallon of ice cream in my lap eating it from the container. I started working with a life coach and began learning how to meal prep healthy meals. I used her method of simple shifts and it was working. She told me to start moving my body, if only a few minutes a day, so I did. I remember the day I got below 300 pounds. I was elated!

After losing around 40 pounds, a coworker mentioned participating in a half marathon. I thought if I did this, I would lose 100 pounds, so I signed up for the race. The training was extensive and I lost another 10 pounds; 50 pounds total. Then, the scale stopped moving. It didn't matter what I did. Weekly I weighed in and the number remained the same. I changed the batteries in the scale. I asked a friend to step on the scale to see if another number would appear. I was in complete disbelief. I had no idea I would over-train and that my body would go into starvation/survival mode and store everything. Some days I would cry or get angry. Then one day, laughter. Then, I realized that I am more than a number. I decided to turn it around. I looked in the mirror and said out loud, "I love you Melissa." Through this plateau, I learned to accept myself. I finally learned through the pain my self-worth, ultimately because the scale wouldn't move.

On race day, I pushed my body to the limit. Looking back, I'm not sure how I did it. I wanted to quit so many times. It would have been easy to get a ride to the finish line. Sheer determination kept me going. Also, proving so many people wrong who told me I couldn't do it or that I was too heavy. Oh yes, no way was I quitting. I would have crawled across that finish line.

I repeated affirmations during the toughest times of the race when I thought about giving up: I deserve this accomplishment. I am worthy of this goal. I am a child of God; He loves me. I was perfectly designed by God for this moment. I love myself. Every day in every way I am getting better and better.

As I was running, other runners were stopping and telling me how strong I was, good job, keep going, don't stop, see you at the finish line. Then I heard my name; it was the running club cheering me on. I felt like a superstar. A little further down was my coworker-turned-friend hanging over the railing screaming my name and saying, "Hell yes! You did it!" A few more strides and I was crossing the finish line. Even more impressive was that I wasn't in last place.

We can do anything we set our minds to. We decide. We commit to that decision with our heart, mind, and soul and we will accomplish our goals.

I'm a 5'3, 265 pound woman who trained for and completed a half marathon and learned to love herself in the process. You my friend, reading this now, can do anything you desire. I accomplished this by believing in myself. Once I started to believe in myself, I became unstoppable.

I believe in you.

MELISSA'S CONFIDENCE TIPS

🎙 Be Grateful – Daily name at least one thing you were grateful for that happened during that day. Your mind will shift to a place of gratitude.

🎙 Speak it into Reality – Visualize your goal. See yourself achieving that goal. Imagine how you will feel when you achieve the goal. Dive into the feeling and remember it.

🎙 Never Give Up – Make a commitment to yourself to achieve your goal and keep going until you reach it.

🎙 Exercise – Move your body for 30 minutes at least three times a week. Remember to drink plenty of water.

🎙 Just Breathe – When life gets overwhelming, take five minutes for yourself to quiet your thoughts and breathe. You will feel refreshed and centered.

🎙 Choose Happiness – Happiness is a decision.

Melissa Tori is a corporate career woman and an entrepreneur who loves helping women find their passion, confidence and self-worth through life lessons, lifting others up and continuing education. Melissa is currently pursuing her dream of becoming a Certified Life Coach, specializing in eldercare and empowering women toward their goals. Melissa is passionate about weight loss and exercise. She believes in the walk-the-walk approach to exercise and weight loss to inspire others to do the same by sharing the ups and downs of her own weight loss journey. Melissa lives in Florida and is the primary caregiver for her elderly mother.

Connect with Melissa
www.MelissaTori.com • FB & IG @MelissaTori

BE CONFIDENT IN YOUR GIFTS

by Angela Merchain

I found my self-confidence and purpose the day I decided to choose my own identity and love and appreciate myself. I am an empath and blessed to have the gift of intuition and healing. I knew I had a special gift since the age of 13 when I was attacked at knifepoint by a home intruder while I was asleep on the sofa; my mom and sister were in the bedroom of our Hollywood apartment. You see, that morning I said to myself, "Today I'm going to die." That was my first premonition. Afterwards, I started to receive messages, see and feel spirits. It did not scare me, as I knew they were trying to communicate with me. Also, I found myself intrigued with the I Ching (The Book of Changes, an ancient Chinese divination text). It's interesting that my mother was actually my number one client when it came to the I Ching, and she not only trusted me, but acted upon my readings. The last reading she acted upon was a home move, which brought upon her many positive life changes.

I finally took ownership of my gifts the day I walked into a crystal shop and received my first chakra energy healing. At first I was unsure about the session I had signed up for, but I was desperate. It was performed by a shaman and he said, "Oh I see all the pain on your right shoulder. You are a giver, but you don't receive much in return." This immediately set me on a new path. People and circumstances that did not serve me as a positive started to dissipate; this was part of the healing process. I took healing, tarot and crystal healing classes by both the shaman and a medium, who helped me understand how to tune into my spirit and intuition. I joined a Raj Yoga Meditation organization that taught me that before anything, I had to learn to love myself. How can I help others if I was sinking? I first had to learn how to swim. Through these practices I learned to be brave, forgiving, accountable, resilient, strong and tolerant. My life changed forever the day I walked into that shop.

A year later, I met a psychic who encouraged me that it was necessary to make my gifts public, as it would help a lot more people. I was scared, as I had become extremely sensitive in the spiritual realm and I could visually see and hear spirits more whether I was awake or asleep, plus self-doubt and fear were so present! Nevertheless, I took her advice. I decided to own my gifts and skills, tore off the Band-Aid and never looked back, because making the difference in someone else's life, and helping others signifies more in my heart. Now, I get to witness how my clients are able to release pain, doubt, loss and move on confidently with their lives. I also understand that no matter how difficult or painful life gets, it's okay, it's part of our journey, and you have to bless it. I know I have to because it has led me to a better and more confident version of myself and you!

I want to share a Meditative Practice.

Find a place within your space where you can mediate every day. Sit on a chair with your arms resting on your legs and the palms of your hands facing up. Inhale and exhale 3 times. With every inhale, tighten your body, and then exhale out. Next, imagine divine light coming in through your crown chakra, going down through your spine, down to your base chakra and attach a grounding cord (any color) to the base chakra and picture this cord going down to the center of the earth. Give your body permission to release all stagnant energy that does not belong to you; to go down this cord to the center of mother earth and ask her to transmute this energy into a violet flame. Now form yourself a gold protective shield that is arm's length around your body. Envision a rose of any color in front of you. Fill up the rose with any thoughts, ideas, emotions, invalidations, circumstances, self-doubt and energy that does not belong or serve you. Once the rose is full, imagine a golden bubble around it and see it drift away into the universe and blow up. Believe that all in that rose is gone, as its energy was received by Mother Nature and transmuted into positive energy.

ANGELA'S INSPIRATION TIPS

🎙️ Always follow your gut, there is a reason why it is our sacral chakra.

🎙️ We all have a contract before coming into this world, not everything needs to make sense, it is okay to let go and go with the flow.

🎙️ Best time to meditate is from 3am to 5am, even if it's 5 minutes. Try it for a week and witness the positive changes.

🎙️ Readings should be done no sooner than 3 months apart – you want to make your independent decisions.

🎙️ Lighter colored crystals such as Amethyst, Citrine and high vibration crystal like Labrodite should be used in calm serene spaces, when meditating or manifesting.

🎙️ Always send "Good Wishes" no matter the circumstance.

 **Angela Merchain's** personality and energy shines through when she steps into a room. She spent 4 years in the educational field and over 20 years as a successful Human Resources professional. However, it was through a life changing experience when she was turned on to the Spiritual Realm and surrendered herself to her God-given gifts. Presently, Angela practices energy healing work, intuitive tarot readings and offers meditative practices to her clients. Through her gifts and love for others, she turns uncertainties into a world of possibilities for her clients and those she cares about.

Connect with Angela
IG @Pure_Balance_ • LinkedIn.com/in/AMerchain444

STEP OUT OF YOUR COMFORT ZONE AND STEP INTO YOU

by Jazzy Juice

What makes you uncomfortable? Public Speaking? Trying something new? Change? At one point in my life, all three made me cringe. If I told those who know me that I used to be shy on the mic, they would laugh at the thought!

I can recall being in grade school and having to speak in front of my class – I would freeze. I can specifically remember one incident in 3rd grade. I was so eager to raise my hand if I knew the answer. My teacher, Mrs. Gilbert-Shapiro, would call on me and if I froze, she would call me out for it. She had a funny sense of humor and although I didn't appreciate it at the time, I am so very grateful that she did that because it lit a fire in me to be a better public speaker, which is much different than just talking to your friends in class.

I started practicing how to speak with confidence. I looked at myself in the mirror and saw how I looked when I spoke. I began to slowly become comfortable with myself. I noticed the way my wild curly hair looked, the way I would smile if I got nervous, the sound of my voice, and the way my lips would purse if I didn't know how to pronunciate a new vocabulary word. Little did I know that I was preparing myself for where my life would take me.

At a young age, I knew that I had to step out of my comfort zone if I wanted to step into the someone I wanted to be. I've stumbled, fallen, gotten back up and taught myself a few things along the way.

Get comfortable getting uncomfortable. Your heart may race and you might get sweaty, clammy and dizzy. These are symptoms of anxiety. Ask yourself if you can feel your feet and take a few deep, cleansing breaths. Look around, what do you see? What do you hear? Practice the art of staying present.

These few steps can help alleviate some anxiety symptoms.

Challenge yourself. You've heard the phrase, *"Fake it 'til you make it."* Well, I say, don't fake it, I say go out there and just do it! Make a list of all the things you've always wanted to try. Some people call it a "Bucket List," I like to call it a "Live It List." If there is something you have always wanted to try, NOW is the time to plan, to *LIVE IT,* and make it possible.

Sometimes you can't "see the big picture," and that's OK! I don't think I ever would have imagined becoming a Jazz & Blues singer or even hosting my own Radio Show! It just happened. Don't limit yourself simply because you can't see the big picture. You too, might be pleasantly surprised by the outcome of your life.

Where thoughts go, energy flows. Create a vision board and write positive affirmations on sticky notes and post them on your bathroom mirror, or anywhere you'll see them every day. Vision boards are fun to make and empowering to see when they come to fruition.

Small daily changes are easier to attain than the dramatic overnight ones. Don't worry. You can, and will, still get there!

Try something new; don't be afraid. It can be very exciting and quite liberating changing what you like, how you want to dress and what you eat. It's just another version of you that you haven't yet experienced. So, go on and STEP OUT OF YOUR COMFORT ZONE AND STEP INTO YOU!

JAZZY'S TIPS

🎤 Decide you want to try something new – Remember, it's OK to start small.

🎤 List the things you want to change – You can write it down on paper or create a vision board. It can be physical or on your electronic device.

🎤 Create a plan to execute that change – Asking for feedback and help from people you trust can be a good start.

🎤 Put together a support group – This is vital to your success. Online groups have been successful for me; I've developed my "tribe" online and it's been AMAZING!

🎤 Journal – I have been journaling for years. It's a positive way to release your thoughts, the good, the bad and the ugly. You don't have to save it.

🎤 Meditate/Pray – Meditating can be as simple as a few deep, cleansing breaths. Praying for guidance in whatever it is you're seeking is powerful in change.

🎤 Be gentle with yourself – If you get off track or fall back into old habits, it's OK! Forgive yourself. No one is perfect. Reach out to that support group you created.

Jazzy Juice is an Intuitive Medium, artist, Jazz & Blues singer and former radio host. She was born in Hollywood, California and was raised in the San Fernando Valley, where she became a wife and mother of two adult children. She currently lives with her Husband and two dogs, Honey and Ziggy.

Connect with Jazzy
IG @Vegan_Diva

Take
ACTION
to reach your
DESTINY!

~ Susie Augustin

ABOUT THE AUTHORS

Susie Augustin is an award-winning speaker and author of many #1 bestselling books, and founder of Get Branded Press. She is known for her Sexy, Fit and Fab™ books and brand, and her Writing to Wow! series. She is an editor and publisher, as well as an expert copywriter with over 25 years experience in the beauty industry with top multi million dollar companies. Susie is a beauty and branding expert, life and business coach, and has trained hundreds of beauty professionals. She is known for using art, creativity and imagination to accentuate her workshops, meetings, and projects. Susie and Kim teach Speaking & Writing to Wow! Workshops, helping entrepreneurs brand themselves as experts through speaking and writing books. Kim and Susie also host two web series, Inspirational Influencers and Passion Power Confidence. With an acting and theatre background, Susie has guest starred in the media often.

Facebook.com/SexyFitFab
@SexyFitFab
#SexyFitFab
#SexyCollaboration
www.SexyFitFab.com

Kim Somers Egelsee has been a speaker for over 25 years, has her degree in speech from CSULB, is a multi award winning Tedx Speaker, and has spoken at over 350 events, meetings and workshops. She has lead, hosted and planned hundreds of events, including the launch of Lessons From Network. Kim is a #1 bestselling author that has also co-authored 11 books, and has shared the stage with greats like Dennis Waitley, Niurka, Brian Tracy, Darren Hardy, Vic Johnson and more. She is a Confidence Consultant and leader of The Exude Confidence Movement. Kim and Susie host two web series, Inspirational Influencers and Passion Power Confidence, and Kim is co-host of Talk Purpose and Truth podcast. Kim is also a business and life coach and leads mastermind groups. With an acting and theatre background, Kim has hosted, acted, and guest starred on various TV shows.

Facebook.com/KimLifeCoach
@KimLifeCoach
#KimLifeCoach
#TenPlusLife
www.KimLifeCoach.com

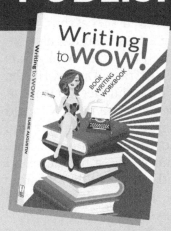

LIVE IN YOUR FULL POSITIVE POWER!

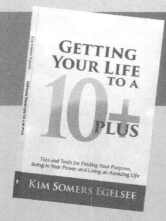

Tips and Tools for finding your purpose, being in your power and living an amazing life!

A powerful how-to book for anyone wanting more happiness, success, and balance in their life. This book gives you the wisdom, stories, and exercises that guide you into self-exploration and positive powerful ways to change your life right away.

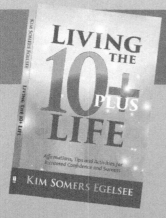

Are you ready to exude confidence in every aspect of your life?

Affirmations, Tips and Activities for increased confidence and success will add bold energy to your life! Create your own opportunities and jump into them, ask for what you want, take action, and live a spectacular *10+ Life!* Amp up your confidence today!

KIM SOMERS EGELSEE
AUTHOR • SPEAKER

SŌL-BALANCE
Mary Sushinski

Join the Sōl-Balance Community to Transform Your Daily Life!

☼ **FOOT ZONE –** Treats the physical, mental and emotional feature of the body by using massage zones of feet.

☼ **EMOTION CODE –** Feel freer, happier and healthier with muscle testing that identifies and releases hidden trapped emotions.

☼ **QUANTUM HEALING –** Activate and align the energy centers to cleanse, charge and source the Life Force Energy.

☼ **ESSENTIAL OILS –** Curating custom blends to raise personal frequency and uplift mood.

☼ **ARTISAN JEWELRY –** Utilizing various materials to hand craft vintage aesthetics and contemporary designs.

SPEAKING ENGAGEMENTS • INTERACTIVE WORKSHOPS

Connect with Mary Sushinski to present Impactful Techniques that Motivate and Inspire Authentic Transformation to Enrich Daily Life.

Connect with Mary at
www.Sol-Balance.com

Kandice Astamendi
SPEAKER • AUTHOR • SALES

CONNECTION • VISIONING • INSPIRATION
Helping People Stay Positive and Powerful in the Face of Adversity.

SPEAKING TOPICS

- How to stay Positive & Powerful in the face of Adversity
- Balance being Strong & Fearless with being Vulnerable & Authentic
- Create your Vision, Create the Life you Love
- Harness your Essence with Inspirational Jewelry

**To Book Kandice to Speak
at your Event and for Interviews**
Contact: **koolpx@yahoo.com**
Or Visit: **www.Kandice98.OrigamiOwl.com**

TraveLynn$_2$

Where your body, mind and soul
meet freedom, connection and adventure.

Experience customized excursions, cultural events,
retreats and dining at amazing discounts.

You name the experience – we'll take you there.

VIP Travel Memberships at Wholesale Prices
- Customize and check off your bucket list
- High-end travel
- Athletic trips
- Humanitarian / Voluntourism trips
- Family friendly trips
- **New!** Elite Travel *(private jets & yachts)*

Book Lynn Heubach, Dream Vacation Specialist to Speak at Your Event

Topics
- How Travel Affects your Body, Mind & Soul
- 7 Tips to Planning your Travel Adventures
- Vision Board Mapping your Dream Vacation
- How Student Exchange Builds Confidence and Courage
- Customized Presentations

Visit Lynn's website for more information **www.TraveLynn2.com**

SPEAK AND WRITE FOR SUCCESS

Keynotes, Workshops, Breakouts, Retreats, Seminars

Speak at Your Event • Host / Emcee
Conduct Workshops • Corporate Coaching
Guest Blogger • Interviews • Web Series Guest
Podcast Guest • Radio Guest

KIM SOMERS EGELSEE AND SUSIE AUGUSTIN

LEARN HOW YOU CAN FIND, EMBRACE AND UTILIZE YOUR OWN POWER FOR SUCCESS IN BUSINESS AND LIFE!

TOPICS

- Live an Exceptional Personal, Business and Spiritual Life
- Speaking & Writing to Wow!
- Getting Your Life to a 10 Plus
- Sexy, Fit & Fab at Any Age
- Make Your Brand Come to Life
- Creativity Can Change Your Life
- Discover & Follow Your Passion
- Living in Your Full Positive Power
- Vision Boards / Brand Boards

CONTACT:
Kim@KimLifeCoach • www.KimLifeCoach.com
Susie@SexyFitFab • www.SexyFitFab.com

LET'S CONNECT!

@GetBrandedPress
#InspirationalInfluencers
YouTube – Inspirational Influencers TV

Facebook.com/GetBrandedPress
@GetBrandedPress
#GetBrandedPress
#WritingtoWow
#DreamitWriteitBrandit
www.GetBrandedPress.com

Made in the USA
Columbia, SC
24 November 2019